Making Sense of World Conflicts

Activities and source materials for teachers of English, Citizenship and PSE

Oxfam

Written by Cathy Midwinter

Advisor: Joanna Skelt

Designed by Garth Stewart

Printed by Information Press, Oxford

First published 2005 by Oxfam GB
274 Banbury Road
Oxford OX2 7DZ

ISBN 1 870727 622

Stock code 68181

Oxfam is a Registered Charity No. 202918

Oxfam works with others to find lasting solutions to overcome poverty and suffering.

Printed on environment-friendly paper.

Cover photograph:
Haiti: Boys and men watch from a street corner as a US soldier, his machine gun at the ready, patrols the streets of Port-au-Prince, the capital.
© UNICEF/HQ04-1050/Michael Kamber

Contents

Acknowledgements

With special thanks to the following teachers and their pupils:

Alison Craig, Lawside Academy; Sara Basford, Tasker Milward School; Julia Murphy, Ysgol Tre-gib; Annie Reyburn, Hethersett High School; Marilyn Webster, Sir Thomas Picton School.

Thanks to Richard Evans, Lisyl Hughes, Edward Waller, Peter Walsh and Stuart Wilson for their suggestions.

Many thanks also to Mike Johns for his advice and support.

This publication would not have been possible without support and contributions from many Oxfam staff.

Sources

Facts and figures

Unless otherwise stated, facts and figures in this book come from one of two main sources:

Shattered Lives: The case for tough international arms control, Amnesty International and Oxfam International, 2003

www.controlarms.org, the website of the Control Arms campaign run jointly by Amnesty International, Oxfam GB and IANSA (International Action Network on Small Arms). The site was accessed between November 2003 and November 2004.

Activities and source materials

Websites were accessed between November 2003 and December 2004.

Page 34 'The rules of war: international humanitarian law' was adapted from material on the website of the International Committee of the Red Cross (**www.icrc.org**).

Part of Activity 3.2 was based on an idea from *How do we make peace* (Discussing global issues series) Unicef UK, 2004.

Information and statistics in the three country profiles (Afghanistan page 65, Rwanda page 44 and Timor Leste page 81) were adapted from the 'World Guide' on the GEsource website (**www.gesource.ac.uk**).

Page 46 'Source B: Reasons for the Rwandan genocide' was adapted from an article by Donny Dithato in *Mmegi/The Reporter* (Gaborone), 7 April 2004.

Page 57 'Gangs and guns: who takes the rap?' was adapted from the website of BBC Manchester (**www.bbc.co.uk/manchester**).

'Corneille's French R 'n' B' on page 68 was adapted from the website of Radio France Internationale (**http://musique.com/siteEn**).

'Mothers' war on gangland shootings' on page 92 was taken from the website of BBC News (**http://news.bbc.co.uk**).

Page 94 'Viva Rio, Brazil' is adapted from the website of Viva Rio (**www.vivario.org.br**).

Page 100 'War and peace journalism' is adapted from *Peace Journalism – How to do it* by Jake Lynch and Annabel McGoldrick (**www.mediachannel.org/originals/warandpeace2.shtml**). A version of this activity was published in *Global Express* no 26 © DEP (Manchester Development Education Project Ltd).

Page 102 'Appendix: Teaching controversial issues' is based loosely on an article by the author, Cathy Midwinter, which was first published in *PSHE and Citizenship Update* issue 27 in May 2003 by Optimus Publishing (**www.optimuspub.co.uk**).

The Publisher wishes to thank the following for their kind permission to reproduce extracts in this book:

Chapter 1: Page 13 Diagram 'Armed conflicts 1990–2001' from *The Atlas of War and Peace*, Dan Smith, Earthscan, 2003 © Myriad Editions Ltd / **www.MyriadEditions.com**.

Chapter 2: Page 25 'Proverbs about conflict from around the world,' Educators for Social Responsibility, **www.esrnational.org/sp/we/uw/proverbs.htm**. Page 33 'My City' by John O'Connor, was quoted by David Rovics on **www.davidrovics.com**.

Chapter 3: Page 41 'The People of the Other Village', from SPLIT HORIZON: *Poems* by Thomas Lux. Copyright © 1994 Thomas Lux. Reprinted by permission of Houghton Mifflin Company. All rights reserved.

Chapter 5: Page 66 'Juma's story' from the website of Save The Children UK (**www.savethechildren.org.uk**). Page 67 'The hawk prays for peace' is reproduced by kind permission of the author Tanure Ojaide; published in *New Poets of West Africa*, Malthouse Press, 1995. Page 67 'Luck in Sarajevo' by Izet Saraljić from *Scar on the stone: Contemporary poetry from Bosnia*, ed. Chris Agee, © Chris Agee, Bloodaxe Books, 1998. Page 67 'Boy with Orange (Out of Kosovo)' from *The Phantom Lane*, Lotte Kramer, Rockingham Press, 2000. Page 68 'Alone in the world' English translation of *Seul au monde* C/A: Corneille © Level Music Inc by kind permission of UNIVERSAL MUSIC PUBLISHING, France. Page 70 'A boy called "Grenade"' from *Letters Home* by Fergal Keane, copyright © Fergal Keane 1999. Page 73 'Shoot now, think later', *The Guardian* © Armando Ianucci 28 April 2003.

Chapter 6: Pages 82–83 'Keeping the peace in Timor Leste 1999' adapted from *Global Express* issue 16, East Timor, September 1999 © DEP (Manchester Development Education Project Ltd). Page 85 'What is Peace?' is from *How do we make peace?* (Discussing Global Issues series) Unicef UK, 2004. Page 85 'Grief' © Ben Okri, first published in *Poems for refugees*, Vintage, 2000.

Chapter 7: Page 91 'Children's radio in Sierra Leone' from the website of Plan UK(**www.plan-uk.org**). Page 92 *A Mother to her Children* is reproduced by kind permission of Black Information Link (**www.blink.org.uk**). Page 98 'Action Card Game' is from *Get Global: A skills-based approach to active global citizenship. Key stages 3 & 4* © ActionAid, 2003.

Every effort has been made to contact copyright holders of material reproduced in this book. Any omissions will be rectified in subsequent printings if notice is given to the publisher.

Oxfam and global citizenship

Oxfam's development education programme aims to create an audience of young people receptive to concepts of global citizenship.

One of the key educational concepts on which *Making Sense of World Conflicts* is based is that of global citizenship. In Oxfam's view, global citizenship goes beyond simply knowing that we are citizens of the globe to an acknowledgement of our responsibilities both to each other and to the Earth itself. It is about valuing the Earth as precious and unique, and safeguarding the future for those coming after us. It includes understanding the need to tackle injustice and inequality, and having the desire and ability to do so actively. Global citizenship is an outlook on life that everyone can have, at any age, anywhere in the world.

Oxfam's *Curriculum for Global Citizenship* gives a framework for the skills, knowledge, values and attitudes which can enable young people to grow up as global citizens, and is summarised below. To find out more about *A Curriculum for Global Citizenship* see **Resources and further reading** on pages 108–110.

The key elements for responsible global citizenship		
Knowledge and understanding	**Skills**	**Values and attitudes**
Social justice and equity	Critical thinking	Sense of identity and self-esteem
Diversity	Ability to argue effectively	Empathy
Globalisation and interdependence	Ability to challenge injustice and inequalities	Commitment to social justice and equity
Sustainable development	Respect for people and things	Concern for the environment and commitment to sustainable development
Peace and conflict	Co-operation and conflict resolution	Belief that people can make a difference

Making Sense of World Conflicts aims to increase pupils understanding of how today's world works, and can be used to support the development of pupils as global citizens in a number of ways. It will help:

- develop *knowledge and understanding* of the way conflict arises and how it affects the lives of people around the world
- enhance *skills* in reading, understanding and comparing different kinds of texts, for example, in order to distinguish fact from opinion
- promote *values and attitudes* relevant to the creation of a more peaceful world, for example, by illustrating how destructive conflict can be to people's security and prosperity, and how important it is that it is resolved without violence.

Why learn about conflict?

The aims of this handbook are to enable teachers and pupils:

- to examine, discuss and tackle in an informed, open and positive way the challenging issues raised by armed conflict in today's world
- to have the confidence and the tools to look at contentious issues and examine contemporary conflicts.

As you read this, there are at least 30 armed conflicts in the world. In today's conflicts, most of the people who are killed are civilians, and almost half of those casualties are children.

At the beginning of the 21st century, conflict issues have been at the top of the agenda of contemporary concerns. Pupils and their teachers have grappled with the complexities of understanding acts of terrorism, mass killings in Sudan, and wars in Afghanistan and Iraq. Other armed conflicts, such as those in Uganda and the Philippines, seem forgotten and remote but as globalisation gathers pace we cannot ignore the increasing arms trade and the impact of armed conflict on our world today.

This book is an element in Oxfam's efforts to achieve its goal of reducing conflict and thereby reducing poverty. Directly and indirectly, armed conflict causes and worsens poverty. *Making Sense of World Conflicts* aims to help teachers and pupils think deeply and creatively about conflict, its causes and effects, and what can be done about it. In doing this, it tries to highlight the relationship between armed conflict and poverty, to show how the prevalence of small arms affects poor countries more than richer ones, and to highlight some of the less-well known conflicts, such as those that took place in Timor Leste (East Timor) and Rwanda.

Conflict and the curriculum

Making Sense of World Conflicts is aimed primarily at teachers of English and Media Studies, with many activities also suitable for Citizenship (in England and Scotland) and PSE (in Wales). Some activities are also suitable for use in Humanities. Conflict in its broadest sense is a topic which English teachers already explore with their pupils through poetry and other literary works. It is an unavoidable part of human life. We have to learn to manage personal and interpersonal conflict, conflict between groups and conflicts in society. Oxfam hopes that this resource will help teachers explore aspects of contemporary armed conflict and thereby supplement their pupils' knowledge and understanding of conflict generally. The activities in this book foster skills such as critical thinking, persuasive writing, reading literary and non-literary texts, and speaking and listening. They will also help pupils to make connections between contemporary conflicts and other conflicts they may have studied, such as the First World War.

In this book Oxfam is using the word 'conflict' to mean armed conflict at any level. This includes international war and also civil war, insurgency, guerrilla war, low-level fighting in the aftermath of conflict and violence in communities.

How to use this book

This book is designed for teachers of pupils aged 14 to 17. It can be used in a flexible way as it presents **source material** and suggests **activities**. Teachers may select particular activities and use the suggested source material, or can use the source material to develop or enhance their own ideas for activities. Suggestions are given for **further work** including possibilities for doing research. These suggestions will lend themselves to the development of **coursework**.

As with other titles in the *Global Issues for Secondary Schools* series, it is not assumed that teachers or pupils will have background knowledge of the places referred to, or of the issues tackled. **Case studies** are used to highlight the causes and effects of conflict and bring the issues to life. Case studies also show how people are resolving conflict and working together to create more peaceful communities. There are suggestions for finding additional sources of information in the further work sections and in the **Resources section** at the back.

Although we see conflict on our televisions every day, the politics and economics of conflicts in other continents may seem distant and obscure. Yet only a moment's reflection is needed to link our own experiences with these events in the news and bring the issues of conflict and gun control closer to home – a report in the local paper of an armed crime, a security delay to a flight from a local airport, a child from a war-torn country new to the school. This resource provides pupils with the **opportunity to link** their own experiences to global events.

Conflict inevitably raises many **controversial issues**. Learning how to explore and discuss controversial issues is an important element in achieving high standards of reading, writing, speaking and listening. It is also a central element of becoming an informed and active global citizen. Suggestions for approaches to teaching controversial issues are offered in the **Appendix** on page 102.

Curriculum opportunities

Making Sense of World Conflicts gives teachers opportunities to fulfil curriculum requirements for English and Citizenship in England, and English and PSE in Wales. Links are also given for Scotland. Many of the activities are also relevant to the Humanities/Social subjects. Below is a summary of the skills that are developed through the activities in the book. A selection of curriculum links for each nation follows on pages 10–12.

English

The source material and activities provide opportunities to:

- explore social and moral issues through contemporary texts, including poetry and non-fiction texts
- support innovative and creative approaches to the theme of conflict using relevant, unusual and challenging texts
- create stimulating ways for pupils to explore how people make sense of difficult experiences through language and image
- use and analyse complex features of language
- assess pupils' contributions to group discussions and interaction.

There are activities for:

- reading, speaking and listening, writing, drama.

There are opportunities for pupils to:

- compare and synthesise information from different texts
- analyse how meaning is conveyed in texts that include print and images
- evaluate the way language is used and how choice of form, layout and presentation contribute to effect
- distinguish between fact and opinion, bias and objectivity
- evaluate how the nature and purpose of media texts influence content and meaning
- develop reading of print and ICT-based information texts.

Citizenship/PSE

There are activities to ensure:

- knowledge and understanding about becoming informed citizens
- development of skills of enquiry and communication
- participation and responsible action.

The source material and activities provide opportunities to:

- think about and discuss political and moral issues and problems arising from events
- discuss some of the wider issues and challenges of global interdependence and responsibility
- look at the work of community-based, national and international voluntary groups
- look at the importance of resolving conflict fairly
- raise issues of human rights and responsibilities and of the importance of a free press and the media's role in society
- make connections between what is learnt in formal settings and experiences in the wider world; acting locally and thinking globally
- make connections in memorable and enjoyable ways
- empower pupils to participate in their communities as active citizens and to develop a global perspective.

Humanities/Social subjects

There are activities for:

- investigation, analysis and interpretation, evaluation, communication.

The source material and activities provide opportunities to:

- develop understanding of moral, ethical, social and cultural issues
- look at a case study of conflict at international level
- consider political, social and economic causes and effects of conflict.

There are opportunities for pupils to look at the following ideas:

- Conflict between groups within a society can have a range of causes and effects.
- Individuals and groups may use different methods in order to resolve conflict and to achieve co-operation.
- The causes and effects of conflict at either a national or international level can differ and affect individuals, groups and societies.
- Individuals, groups, nations and international organisations can play a role in resolving conflict.
- Individuals and groups have experienced and continue to experience prejudice and persecution and there are various causes.
- Individuals, groups, nations and international organisations can act to reduce or resolve prejudice and persecution.
- Societies contain interest groups with different views about their organisation and resources.
- Democracy allows differences in society to be resolved fairly and peacefully.

Geography

There are opportunities for pupils to develop awareness of the ways in which armed conflict affects development due to the impact, challenges and constraints on people, places and environments, and their interaction.

History

There are opportunities for pupils studying 20th-century and contemporary history to carry out activities related to case studies of international relations, the UN and the conduct of armed conflict.

Religious Education

There are opportunities for pupils to discuss the values of truth, justice, respect for all and diversity in society through understanding similarities and differences, and the changing nature of society. Through the activities they can interpret and evaluate a variety of responses, recognise the complexity of issues, weigh up opinions, and make judgements supported by a range of evidence.

National Curriculum Orders: England

Below is an overview of how this resource links to the curriculum requirements at Key Stages 3 and 4 in England. We have not given the links for every activity, but have indicated which areas are covered most in this book.

English

Speaking and Listening

Knowledge, skills and understanding – especially	Group discussion and interaction	3 a) b) c) d) e)
	Drama	4 a)
	Speaking	8 a) b) c)
	Listening	9 a) b) c)
Breadth of study – especially	Group discussion and interaction	10 a) b)
	Drama activities	11 a)

Reading

Knowledge, skills and understanding – especially	Understanding texts	1 a) b) c) d)
	Texts from different cultures and traditions	3 d) e)
	Printed and ICT-based information texts	4 a) b) c)
	Media and moving image texts	5 a) b) c) d)
Breadth of study – especially	Literature	8 a) v, vi, c)
	Non-fiction and non-literary texts	9 b) c)

Writing

Knowledge, skills and understanding – especially	Composition	1 i) j) k) l) m) n)
	Planning and drafting	2 c)
Breadth of study – especially	Range of purposes	9 c) d) 10

Citizenship

Knowledge, skills and understanding about becoming informed citizens

Pupils should be taught about:

1 a) the legal and human rights underpinning society

1 f) the work of community-based, national and international voluntary groups and the opportunities for individuals and voluntary groups to bring about social change locally, nationally and internationally

1 g) the importance of resolving conflict fairly

1 h) the importance of a free press and the media's role in society, including the internet, in providing information and affecting opinion

1 i) the world as a global community, and the political, economic, environmental and social implications of this, and the role of ... the United Nations

1 j) the wider issues and challenges of global interdependence and responsibility

Developing skills of enquiry and communication

Pupils should be taught to:

2 a) think about and research topical political, spiritual, moral, social and cultural issues, problems and events by analysing information and its sources, including ICT-based sources

2 b) justify orally and in writing a personal opinion about such issues, problems or events

2 c) contribute to group and exploratory class discussions, and take part in debates

Developing skills of participation and responsible action

Pupils should be taught to:

3 a) use their imagination to consider other people's experiences and be able to think about, express, explain and critically evaluate views that are not their own

National Curriculum Orders: Wales

Below is an overview of how this resource links to the curriculum requirements for English and PSE in Wales. To save space we have given the links at Key Stage 4 for English; those for Key Stage 3 are very similar. The PSE links are an ammalgamation of Key Stages 3 and 4.

English Key Stage 4		
Oracy	Range	
	Skills	1,2,3,4,5
Reading	Range	1, 2, 3
	Skills	1, 2, 3, 4, 5, 7, 8, 9, 10, 11, 12
	Language development	1, 2, 5
Writing	Range	1, 2, 5
	Skills	1, 2
	Language development	1, 10

Personal and Social Education Framework	
Attitudes and values	• Consider the deeper questions in life and the search for meaning and purpose.
	• Be moved by injustice, exploitation and denial of human rights.
	• Develop a sense of personal responsibility towards the environment and a concern for the quality of life both in the present and the future.
Skills	• Listen attentively in different situations and respond appropriately.
	• Communicate confidently and effectively one's feelings and views in a wide range of situations and maintain with conviction a personal standpoint.
	• Appreciate, reflect on and critically evaluate others' viewpoints and messages from the media.
	• Empathise with others' experiences and feelings.
	• Use a range of techniques for personal reflection.
	• Use a range of strategies to resolve conflict with a win/win situation.
	• Adapt to changing situations.
	• Make decisions and choices effectively.
	• Make reasoned moral judgements and resolve moral issues and dilemmas.
	• Review and reflect on learning and analyse strengths and weaknesses.
	• Work both independently and co-operatively.
	• Take part in debates and vote on issues.
Knowledge and understanding	• Understand cultural differences; recognise and know how to challenge expressions of prejudice and stereotyping.
	• Understand the nature of local, national and international communities with reference to cultural diversity, justice, law and order and interdependence.
	• Know how democratic systems work and understand how individual citizens, public opinion, lobby groups, and the media can contribute and have an influence and impact.
	• Have a developing global awareness of contemporary issues and events including human rights and sustainable development.
	• Have insight into their beliefs and values in the context of those in society and propagated by the media.
	• Know how their beliefs and values affect their identity and lifestyle.
	• Recognise moral issues and dilemmas in life situations and be aware of the factors involved in making moral judgements.
	• Know what they believe to be right and wrong actions and understand the issues involved.
	• Identify a set of values and principles by which to live.

National Qualifications Framework: Scotland

Below is an overview of how this resource links to the National Course Requirements for Standard Grade, Intermediate and Higher English; to the relevant National Priority in Education; and to the Education for Citizenship Framework.

English

Standard grade

Reading	• to obtain particular information from a text
	• to grasp ideas or feelings implied in a text
	• to evaluate the writer's attitudes, assumptions and argument
	• to appreciate the writer's craft
	• to enjoy and obtain enrichment from a text
Writing	• to convey information
	• to deploy ideas, expound, argue and evaluate
	• to describe personal experience, express feelings and reactions
	• to employ specific literary forms (eg short story, letter, poem)
Listening	• to obtain particular information from a message
	• to grasp ideas or feelings implied in a message
	• to evaluate the attitudes, assumptions and arguments expressed in a message
	• to appreciate the techniques used in a message
Talking	• to convey information
	• to deploy ideas, expound, argue and evaluate
	• to describe personal experience, express feelings and reactions
	• to create particular effects

Intermediate 2, Higher

Approaches to teaching and learning	• Exploring, in talk and writing, experiences (both real and imagined), feelings, emotions and ideas.
	• Expressing these in a variety of prose/dramatic/poetic forms.
	• Taking part in debates.
	• Undertaking personal reading, independent study and research.
	• Skimming, scanning, close reading.
	• Consulting and comparing a number of texts.
	• Contrasting and collating information from different texts.
	• Acquiring awareness of the contexts (literary, historical, ideological, for example) of a text.
	• Forming opinions and taking a stance.
Literature	Writings from other cultures in the English-speaking world and, where appropriate, works in translation.

National Priorities in Education: Scotland

Priority Four – Values and Citizenship

To work with parents to teach pupils respect for self and one another and their interdependence with other members of their neighbourhood and society and to teach them the duties and responsibilities of citizenship in a democratic society.

Education for Citizenship Framework

Knowledge and understanding – especially

Young people should demonstrate an understanding of:	• contemporary local and global issues, paying regard to available evidence, and to a range of ideas and interpretations of their significance
	• the rights and responsibilities underpinning democratic and other societies
	• the causes of conflict and possible approaches to resolving it
	• global interdependence

Skills and competences – especially

Young people should become more able to:	• locate, handle, use and communicate information and ideas, using ICT as appropriate
	• question and respond constructively in debate and/or in writing
	• contribute to discussions and debate in ways that are assertive and, at the same time, attentive to and respectful of others' contributions
	• make informed decisions in relation to political, community and environmental issues

Values and dispositions – especially

Young people should become more disposed to:	• develop informed and reasoned opinions about political, economic, social and environmental issues
	• express, explain and critically evaluate views that are not their own
	• understand and value social justice, recognising that what counts as social justice is itself contentious

Creativity and enterprise – especially

Young people should become more able to:	• identify and frame their own questions and problems and suggest possible solutions
	• respond in imaginative ways to social, moral and political dilemmas and challenges
	• imagine alternatives to current ways of doing things

Armed conflict: the issues

Since the end of the Cold War in 1989, there have been more than 120 wars worldwide. Initial hopes in the North that after the Cold War there would be a new era of peace fell away as brutal conflicts raged in the South, in the former Soviet Union, and in the Balkans. In the mid-1990s the number of armed conflicts increased sharply and our awareness of them grew, but since the turn of the century the annual total has begun to decrease.

During the Cold War, conflict was usually seen and understood in East–West terms. Alliances and trade in arms related to the two major power blocs – the USA and the Soviet Union. Any conflicts that did not fit that model were almost ignored. Nowadays, however, it is possible to understand each conflict in its own right – as a political problem, human tragedy or humanitarian disaster rather than for its significance in superpower rivalry. It is now more possible to take action to try to end these wars and create a better way of life for the ordinary people of countries caught up in armed conflict.

Nevertheless, the new era is characterised by the USA's overwhelming military predominance. But as the events of 11 September 2001 showed, this does not make the USA invulnerable. Issues of power go hand-in-hand with issues of security. The 'war on terror' has raised new questions about how to understand conflict.

Armed conflicts around the world ▶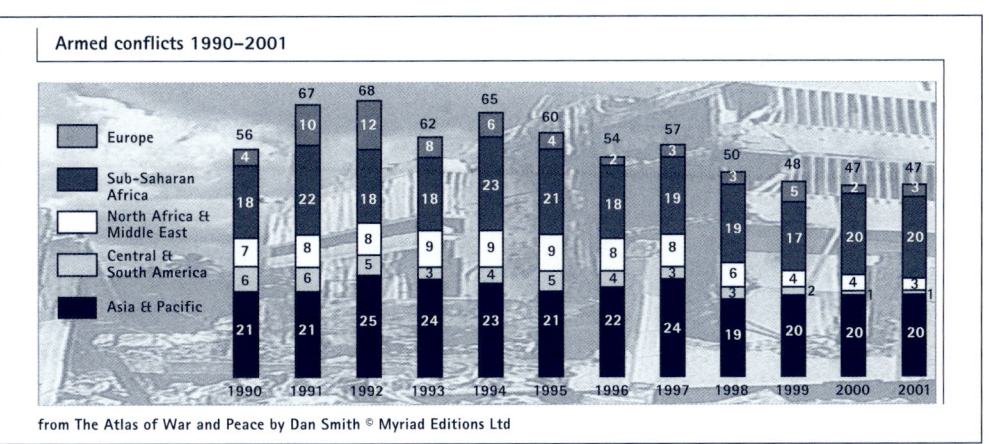

Armed conflicts 1990–2001

from The Atlas of War and Peace by Dan Smith © Myriad Editions Ltd

The causes of conflict

❝ *Fewer than ten per cent of contemporary wars are between states. Wars of independence from colonial power are almost completely a thing of the past, though there are many wars of secession, in which the leaders of one region or ethnic group in a state try to break away from it. International war inevitably gets enormous media coverage, not only because of its evident importance, but also because of its rarity value, but almost all wars today are fought within states rather than between them.* ❞

The Atlas of War and Peace, Dan Smith, Earthscan, 2003.

When thinking about the causes of conflict, it helps to divide them into different types. There are background causes that have built up over a long period with problems that just need a spark to ignite the conflagration. Often these problems entail both poor economic conditions and a lack of ways to seek change peacefully. People in poor countries where democracy is uncertain and leadership uneven often experience growing frustration.

The shorter-term actions of politicians and political movements with their particular goals and almost random triggers – accidents, unforeseen events or sometimes small deliberate acts – can all set conflict in motion.

Wars today are concentrated in the poorest countries. In *Shattered Lives: The case for tough international arms control* (Amnesty International UK and Oxfam International 2003), it is argued that countries become caught in a cycle of poverty and conflict.

> *Arms are one key factor in facilitating, prolonging, and intensifying conflict and armed violence. Arms are used arbitrarily and indiscriminately to kill or injure, to threaten people and drive them from their homes; the flow of arms enables and sustains conflicts in which civilian casualties mount. At a deeper level, the misuse of arms may obstruct the possibilities for development and interfere with people's rights to a decent livelihood, health services, and education.*

The vicious circle of conflict and poverty ▶

Poverty fuels conflict : As per capita income halves, the risk of civil war roughly doubles.*

Conflict fuels poverty : A typical civil war leaves a country 15% poorer, with around 30% more people living in absolute poverty.**

*Development and Peace, Paul Collier in *Global Future, First Quarter 2003* **The global menace of local strife, *The Economist*, 24 May 2003

Shattered Lives/Oxfam

Development means giving people choices, through education and training and through creating an environment for them to develop their full potential and lead productive, creative lives; but this cannot happen when people live in fear of the misuse of arms, whether by state or non-state actors. Human development depends on peace and personal security, and thus sustainable development is a victim of insecurity. Poor development indicators go hand in hand with insecurity and conflict.

Civil war and development ▶

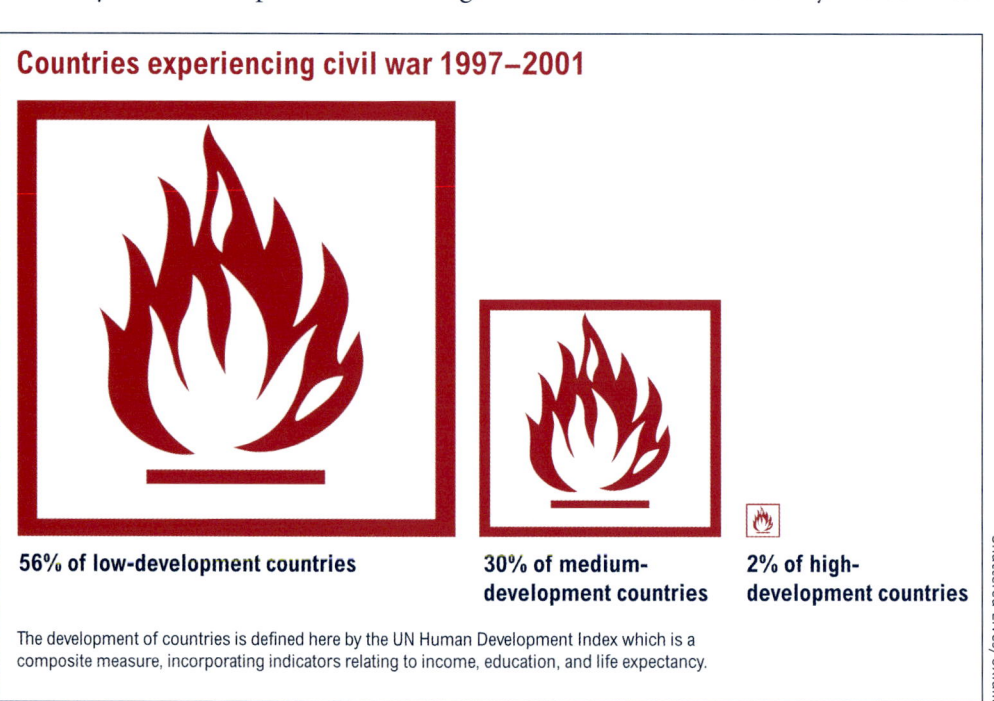

Countries experiencing civil war 1997–2001

56% of low-development countries

30% of medium-development countries

2% of high-development countries

The development of countries is defined here by the UN Human Development Index which is a composite measure, incorporating indicators relating to income, education, and life expectancy.

Shattered Lives/Oxfam

The effects of armed conflict

An average of US$22bn a year is spent on arms by countries in Africa, Asia, the Middle East, and Latin America – a sum that would otherwise enable those same countries to be on track to meet the Millennium Development Goal of achieving universal primary education (estimated at $10bn a year) as well as targets for reducing infant and maternal mortality (estimated at $12bn a year).

Shattered Lives summary

Every day in its work around the world, Oxfam witnesses the abuse of arms which fuels conflict, poverty, and violations of human rights. The impact of the widespread proliferation and misuse of arms is now severe. The effects of armed conflict reach into the lives of men, women and children throughout the world. The direct and indirect impacts of war and violence have already reached a critical point and will become even more significant over the next 20 years, imposing an intolerable burden on poor communities. By 2020, the numbers of deaths and injuries from war and violence could overtake the numbers of deaths caused by killer diseases such as measles and malaria, unless there is concerted action now to reverse current trends.

As already noted, most wars today are fought within nations. Conflicts often involve several different armed forces, sometimes divided along ethnic lines. They usually involve irregular forces fighting in civilian areas. The civilian casualty figures show the impact of these trends. Best estimates are that 14 per cent of total casualties were civilians in the First World War. This increased to 67 per cent in the Second World War, and has grown even higher in many of today's wars.

For example, in the Democratic Republic of Congo and in Colombia the distinction between civilians and combatants is often blurred by the actions of government and illegal armed actors alike. Civilians are used as a cover for military and paramilitary operations, as a shield against air or artillery attacks, and as providers of subsistence, shelter, and sexual gratification – mostly at the point of a gun. They are then attacked in reprisal killings and suffer the denial of material aid. Combatants tend to use civilian infrastructure, telecommunications, and logistics for military purposes – making the distinction between military and civilian targets very difficult.

The violation of human rights

The easy availability of arms tends to increase the incidence of armed violence, prolong wars once they break out, and enable grave and widespread abuses of human rights. In some situations, the escalating supply of arms acts as a *trigger* for conflict. In crime-ridden societies, the easy availability of arms is linked to the level of armed violence. Studies from developed countries (data are rarely available elsewhere) consistently show a clear correlation between household gun ownership and death rates. This link is most clearly seen in the case of suicides and accidental deaths, and especially among young people. Sometimes it is police and other law-enforcement officials who commit armed crime and violate human rights.

How violent crime affects different income groups ▶

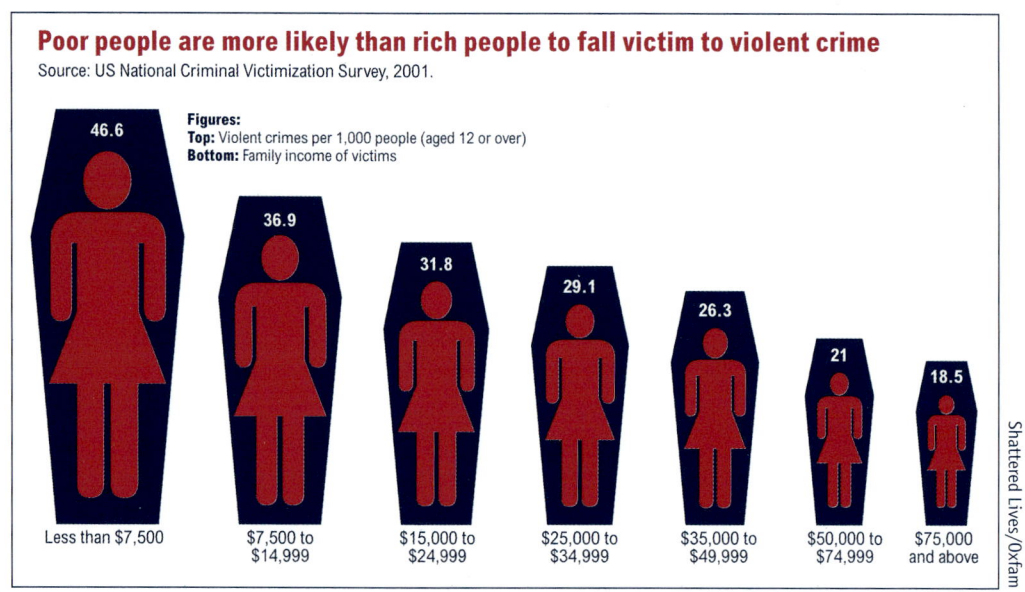

Poor people are more likely than rich people to fall victim to violent crime
Source: US National Criminal Victimization Survey, 2001.

Figures:
Top: Violent crimes per 1,000 people (aged 12 or over)
Bottom: Family income of victims

46.6 — Less than $7,500
36.9 — $7,500 to $14,999
31.8 — $15,000 to $24,999
29.1 — $25,000 to $34,999
26.3 — $35,000 to $49,999
21 — $50,000 to $74,999
18.5 — $75,000 and above

Shattered Lives/Oxfam

Violations of civil and political rights

Torture and arbitrary arrests

Violations take place while people are detained, either in police stations, detention centres or prisons. The statistics are shocking. Between 1997 and 2000, Amnesty International received reports of torture or ill-treatment by state officials in more than 150 countries.

Sexual violence

Armed sexual violence is widespread in heavily armed environments. Weapons can be used to facilitate systematic rape – a war crime, used to hasten the expulsion of national groups by degrading women and spreading terror, fear and humiliation. Sexual violence against men may also be significant, but few data on this type of abuse have so far been collated, and it is believed that most cases are not reported.

The psychological impact

Physical injuries command most attention, yet the psychological burden of armed attack is severe and enduring, though frequently overlooked. Psychiatrists in Croatia working with women who have been raped, bereaved or displaced believe that it will take two to three generations before the psychological effects of the war pass.

Forced to flee

At the end of 2002, there were around 22 million internally displaced people across the world. About 13 million were refugees and asylum-seekers seeking protection outside their own countries. Most of the world's displaced population consists of women and children. Estimates show that 4.3 million people were newly uprooted in 2002, the majority in Africa.

Abduction and hostage-taking

Men, women, and children are abducted at gunpoint and forced to fight or work for their abductors. In Uganda, the Lord's Resistance Army has abducted more than 20,000 children since 1986; children make up a very high proportion of LRA soldiers. Those caught trying to escape are summarily executed, as a warning to others. Between 10,000 and 17,000 women and children have been abducted from southern Sudan.

Violations of social and economic rights

Denial of aid

Armed violence, actual and threatened, prevents aid reaching those who desperately need it. Warring parties may purposely block humanitarian assistance, using access to food and medical supplies as a military tactic. Sometimes aid workers, their convoys, their offices, and their programmes are specifically targeted.

Denial of livelihoods

The means to make a living and provide for a family are affected as armed groups target communities for supplies, or prevent people from engaging in commerce. With assets depleted, people are less and less able to cope with external shocks; repeated disruption poses a severe threat to secure supplies of food. Income falls to such a level that people have to reduce the number of meals they eat, and sell their assets to survive.

Denial of health care

Armed conflict is a hazard to health. Acute health problems cannot be treated if people are denied access to health services. Maternal and child mortality – key indicators for the Millennium Development Goals – increase markedly in contexts of armed violence.

Denial of education

Conflict and armed crime hamper education. Schools are closed in response to danger, damage, and lack of teachers; sometimes schools are appropriated for other purposes, such as housing for displaced people. In larger Brazilian cities, it is not uncommon for classes to be interrupted or schools closed because of gunfire during territorial battles between rival drug gangs or clashes with police.

While most people would accept that some military spending is inevitable, it must be acknowledged that it competes with many aspects of civilian spending – on infrastructure, education, health care, environmental protection, the police, and so on.

The opportunity costs of military spending ▶

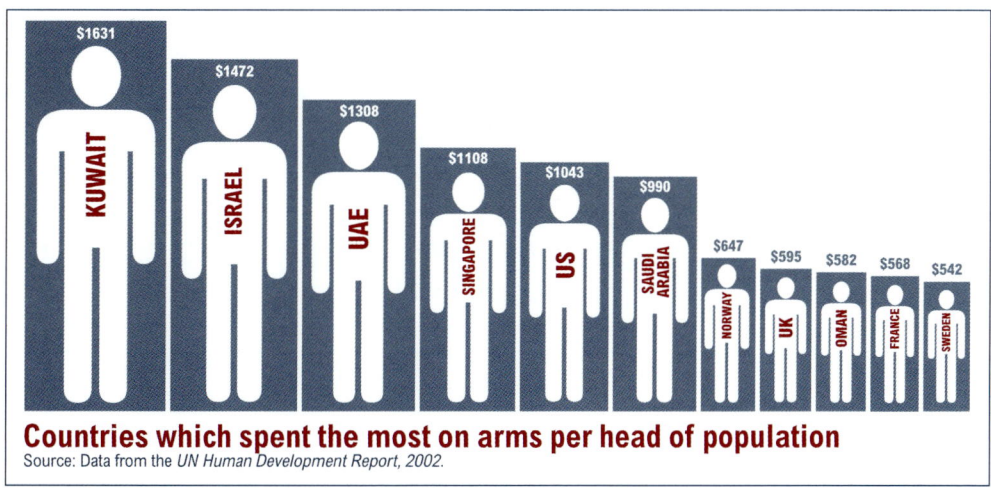

Countries which spent the most on arms per head of population
Source: Data from the *UN Human Development Report, 2002*.

Shattered Lives/Oxfam

The aftermath of armed conflict

After armed conflict, governments tend to keep military spending high, to guard against future insurgency. Military spending consumes on average 2.8 per cent of governments' budgets before conflict, 5 per cent during conflict, and 4.5 per cent in the first decade of peace after civil war. Yet this expenditure is mortgaging a country's development: research shows that money could often be better spent on health care and education, signalling the government's intentions for peace and encouraging private investment.

Economic gains are lost as countries seriously affected by armed violence slide into instability. Trade and production are disrupted, tourists stay away, and state management of infrastructure and national resources may be disrupted. A detailed study estimated the cost of the war in Sri Lanka up to 1998 at a staggering US$20.8 billion – of which 23 per cent was war-related expenditure, 9 per cent related to damages, and 67 per cent stemmed from loss of output. In Africa, the economic losses due to wars are estimated to be US$15 billion per year.

Demobilisation, disarmament, and reintegration programmes are a necessity after the official end of armed conflict. Countries are often flooded with armed former fighters; surplus arms must be taken out of their hands and destroyed, and livelihoods must be restored. In June 2003, there were thought to be 24 million guns in Iraq, enough to arm every man, woman, and child, and they could be purchased for around US$10 each; this has been one factor behind the state of insecurity and acts of lawlessness in the country following the end of the war.

It is not only small arms that are left behind. Landmines, bomblets from cluster bombs, and other unexploded ordnance (UXO) remain well after the official end of conflict, causing between 15,000 and 20,000 new casualties each year, with huge loss of life and permanent disability. Cluster bombs have been a major source of death and injury in Iraq. The presence of landmines and UXO inhibits access to homes and fields, preventing people from restarting their lives and rebuilding their country.

The impact of the widespread proliferation and misuse of arms is now critical. The 'war on terror' should have focused political will to prevent arms falling into the wrong hands. Instead, since the attacks on the World Trade Center and the Pentagon on 11 September 2001, some suppliers have relaxed their controls in order to arm newfound allies against 'terrorism', irrespective of their disregard for international human rights and humanitarian law. Despite the damage that they cause, there is still no binding, comprehensive, international law to control the export of conventional arms.

(This introduction is based on *Shattered Lives: The case for tough international arms control*, Amnesty International UK and Oxfam International, 2003.)

2 What is conflict?

Exploring ideas and analysing image and language

Aims for this chapter:

- To explore perceptions, concepts and contexts of armed conflict
- To develop a conceptual framework for understanding armed conflict.

This chapter introduces pupils to the different definitions of the word 'conflict'. There are a variety of activities and source materials that will enable pupils to explore how they understand and perceive conflict and where these perceptions come from. It is recommended that some time is spent on these activities as conflict is a complex concept and has emotional as well as political, economic and social aspects. It will be important for pupils to explore their own values and attitudes and clarify the many aspects of conflict and how they relate to them.

You might like to keep the results of these activities and look at them again with your pupils at the end of the work on conflict to evaluate the learning that has taken place. They could revisit the activities and assess how their understanding and attitudes may have changed.

If it seems as though some of the activities could be extended or there are questions raised which require more in-depth discussion, there are opportunities in the **Further work and sources** section or in later chapters to pick up the issues.

Activities in this chapter:

- Thinking about conflict – defining conflict
- Considering conflict and culture
- Analysing conflict in the news
- Finding out about armed conflict
- Thinking about terrorism

Activity 2.1

Thinking about conflict – defining conflict

Objectives

- To recognise that the word 'conflict' can have a number of different meanings.
- To clarify what pupils understand by the term 'conflict'.

Learning outcomes

Pupils will have:

- used information processing and reasoning skills
- developed their understanding of the term 'conflict'.

You will need

- Copies for each pair of pupils of the pictures on pages 21–23, cut up separately

Starter

1   Use the source material of pictures relating to conflict on pages 21–23. You can substitute or add pictures that you have found from elsewhere. Give pupils in pairs copies of the pictures, ideally cut up separately.

2   Ask pupils in pairs to rank the pictures in a diamond shape placing the picture that is most like their idea of 'conflict' at the top and the one least like 'conflict' at the bottom.

Activity

3   Ask each pair for their choice of top and bottom picture and make a note on the board. Discuss the outcome and encourage thinking skills by asking pupils to give reasons for their opinions and to use precise language to explain what they think.

4   Make a list on the board of all the different types of conflict that are shown in the pictures or that have been mentioned – brainstorm any others.

5   Discuss possible categories with the class, for example conflict at different levels – internal, interpersonal, community, national or international; verbal conflict, violent conflict or armed conflict. Does categorising conflict help to define it?

6   Ask them in groups of four to write a definition of 'conflict' in not more than 20 words.

7   Each group then displays its definition.

Closing discussion

8   Discuss the definitions. Discuss the reasons why 'conflict' may have a variety of different meanings and the extent to which meaning is dependent on context. Encourage pupils to give examples as evidence for their views.

9   The class could vote on the best definition or come up with a consensus definition.

What is conflict?

1

Andrew Testa/Panos

2

Jenny Matthews

3

Martin Adler/Panos

Making Sense of World Conflicts

What is conflict?

4

Associated Press/Moshe Bursuker

5

The Robin Hood Project, The University of Rochester

6

www.sangrea.net

What is conflict?

7

Sandro Vannini/Corbis

8

Asia Society

9

Imperial War Museum

Making Sense of World Conflicts

Activity 2.2

Considering conflict and culture

Objectives

- To explore, hypothesise, debate and analyse.
- To express a personal opinion about an issue.

Learning outcomes

Pupils will have:

- justified and defended orally a personal opinion
- contributed to exploratory group and class discussions.

You will need

- A copy of 'Proverbs about conflict from around the world' on page 25, for each pair

Proverbs provide wonderful nuggets of discussion-provoking wisdom. Proverbs, while arising out of and illuminating different cultures, also exemplify widely shared truths and help understanding of ideas.

According to the Ghanaian researcher Kofi Asare Opoku, 'The Yoruba of Nigeria emphasise the value of proverbs with a proverb, saying, "A proverb is the horse that can carry one swiftly to the discovery of ideas"'.

Good proverbs are more complex than they may seem at first and can almost always be fruitfully examined, discussed and even reversed. There are many different websites devoted to proverbs from the UK and around the world, for example *African Proverbs, Sayings and Stories* (**www.afriprov.org**).

Starter

1 Talk briefly about what proverbs are – 'a short familiar saying expressing a supposed truth or moral lesson', according to *The Chambers Dictionary* (1993).

2 Brainstorm proverbs that pupils know that relate to conflict in some way; for example, 'Revenge is a dish best served cold' or 'Sticks and stones may break my bones but names will never hurt me'. How much truth do pupils feel these proverbs contain?

Activity

3 Give each pair of pupils a copy of 'Proverbs about conflict from around the world' and ask them to pick out their three favourites.

4 Then each pair of pupils can take a different proverb to discuss and explain to the rest of the class.

5 You can further explore the meanings by asking them to pick out one proverb to fit different categories such as the wisest, the funniest, the weirdest, the most co-operative, the least co-operative, the best advice, the one that illuminates conflict best, or the one that says the most interesting thing about conflict.

6 Discuss the fact that these proverbs come from different cultures. Does conflict in different cultures seem to be viewed in similar or very different ways? Would the proverbs have the same meaning within any culture? Does this tell us anything about the nature of conflict? Pupils could write their own proverbs about conflict or create posters illustrating one or more of the proverbs (as a homework task).

Closing discussion

7 Discuss what these proverbs may teach us about conflict. Are they on the whole advocating revenge or forgiveness, competition or co-operation? Draw some examples of conflict in different cultures from literature that the class is familiar with.

Proverbs about conflict from around the world

1. 'Opinions founded on prejudice are always sustained with the greatest violence.'
Hebrew-language proverb of Israel

2. 'Equality is not easy, but superiority is painful.'
Serere proverb of Senegal, West Africa

3. 'A frog in the well does not know the ocean.'
Proverb of Japan

4. 'Lions believe that everyone shares their state of mind.'
Proverb of Mexico

5. 'The tears running down your face do not blind you.'
Togolese proverb of Togo, West Africa

6. 'When your neighbour is wrong you point a finger, but when you are wrong you hide.'
Ekonda proverb, Democratic Republic of Congo, Central Africa

7. 'If you have one finger pointing at somebody, you have three pointing towards yourself.'
Proverb of Nigeria

8. 'If you damage the character of another, you damage your own.'
Yoruba proverb of Nigeria, West Africa.

9. 'In the desert of life the wise person travels by caravan, while the fool prefers to travel alone.'
Arab proverb, country unspecified, North Africa
(To 'travel by caravan' here means to travel in a group. A caravan was a group of people travelling across the desert.)

10. 'The bridge is repaired only after someone falls in the water.'
Proverb of Somalia, East Africa

11. 'Those who seek revenge must remember to dig two graves.'
Proverb of China

12. 'Without retaliation, evils would one day become extinct from the world.'
Proverb of Nigeria

13. 'The wind does not break a tree that bends.'
Sukuma proverb of Tanzania, East Africa

14. 'A wise person changes their mind.'
Proverb of Japan

15. 'To engage in conflict, one does not bring a knife that cuts – but a needle that sews.'
Adapted from a Bahumbu proverb of Zambia, Southern Africa

16. 'When the right hand washes the left hand and the left hand washes the right hand, both hands become clean.'
Proverb of Nigeria

(Source: Educators for Social Responsibility, www.esrnational.org)

Activity 2.3

Analysing conflict in the news

Objectives

- To research and analyse reported conflict on TV news.
- To use evaluation skills to assess the impact of TV news on an audience.

Learning outcomes

Pupils will have:

- developed their enquiry, analysis and evaluation skills
- reflected on and made judgements about opinions and ideas.

You will need

- A copy of the 'Conflict in the news' activity sheet on pages 27–28 for each pupil for the homework activity

N.B. You will need to set up the research activity in advance of the lesson. Give each pupil a copy of the 'Conflict in the news' activity sheet on pages 27–28, go through the sheet and ask pupils to carry out this activity for homework whilst watching a main TV news broadcast.

Starter

1 Carry out a brainstorm with the class on sources of information about conflict in the world.

2 Carry out a straw poll to see which source pupils think they get most of their information from – this may well be the TV or other media. How many pupils watch the news? What do they think of it? Is it all bad news? Lead into the activity, which will enable them to discuss TV as a source of information in more detail.

Activity

3 Pupils should get into groups and look at the results of their analysis of conflict on TV news discussing any aspects that are surprising. They should look for:

- any similarities or differences in their individual findings
- whether the findings show variations according to the time of the news programme or the channel
- the different types of conflict shown
- which types of conflict featured most often.

4 Each group should choose a method of collating the group (or class) findings and produce a group poster, whether it be a set of bullet points drawing out the key points, a bar chart or a diagram such as a spider diagram.

5 The posters can be displayed and each group should report back to the class.

Closing discussion

6 Discuss the findings with the class, especially the amount of conflict. Was the news informative with regard to the conflict – was the conflict explained and were the reasons for it given? How much violent and armed conflict was shown on the news? Was it important and necessary to show it? How much might the amount of violent and armed conflict shown on TV news affect us? Is it something to worry about? Are there certain things that should not be shown on TV news?

7 Try to come to a consensus on the importance of TV news in informing us about conflict around the world. What are the strengths of this medium and what are its limitations?

Conflict in the news – activity sheet

Time of news programme	
Length of news programme	
TV channel	

PART A   Fill in this part while the news programme is on

1. **How many news stories are about conflict?**
   Write a brief note about each story.
   The stories about conflict are ...

   1.

   2.

   3.

   4.

   5.

   6.

2. **How many times do you see violence occur?**
   Keep track by ticking here each time you see something violent.

3. **What types of conflict are the stories about?** Tick the types of conflict shown. You can tick each type more than once if necessary.

   - war between nations
   - civil war (war within a country)
   - demonstration
   - strike
   - political disagreement
   - football violence
   - terrorism
   - murder
   - other (say what it is) ...

Making Sense of World Conflicts

Conflict in the news – activity sheet

PART B   Fill in this part after the news programme has finished

Choose one news story on conflict and fill in the details below.

4. **Explain what you saw for the news story you have chosen.**

>

5. **How was the conflict in this story portrayed?** Tick one or more.

☐ heroically ☐ emotionally ☐ other
☐ as a terrible thing ☐ factually (say how)
☐ as a good thing ☐ neutrally

6. **How did this story make you feel?** Tick one or more.

☐ confused ☐ excited ☐ shocked
☐ angry ☐ worried ☐ other (give details)
☐ bored ☐ guilty
☐ interested ☐ informed

7. **Write down any thoughts and questions you have about the story.**

>

8. **How much do you think you learnt from the news story you chose?**
☐ no idea ☐ not much ☐ quite a lot ☐ a lot

9. **What did you think of the reporting of the story you chose?**
☐ Good – everything was clear and it was interesting.
☐ It was OK – they tried!
☐ Not very good – it was confusing and it didn't hold my attention.
☐ Other (give details) ...

How could the reporting have been improved?

>

10. **How would you feel about children under ten seeing this news story?**

>

Activity 2.4

Finding out about armed conflict

Objectives

- To explore and extend knowledge about armed conflict.

Learning outcomes

Pupils will have:

- anticipated responses and tested ideas and conclusions
- developed information-processing skills.

You will need

- A copy of the 'Armed conflict quiz' on page 31 for each pupil

Useful sources of information are facts, figures and maps of conflicts such as those to be found on the Peace Pledge Union website: **www.ppu.org.uk**. (Click on 'War facts' and then explore that section.)

Starter

1 Hand out the 'Armed conflict quiz' on page 31 which pupils can do individually or in pairs. Tell them that it is not a test and not to worry if they don't know the answers – they should guess. It is a way of both finding out what they know about conflict in today's world and giving them some information when they get the answers. Give them about ten minutes to do the quiz.

Activity

2 Go through the answers to the quiz and discuss any particular points that need clarifying. Discuss any information that surprised pupils. Were any misconceptions demonstrated through doing the quiz? How do misconceptions arise?

3 Ask pupils what the quiz can tell us about changes in armed conflict. Are armed conflicts more or less likely to affect civilians than in the past? Draw out the point that present-day armed conflicts are far more likely to involve and affect civilians.

4 Brainstorm the armed conflicts that pupils know about that are happening at present.

5 Ask pairs of pupils to research and map or list present-day armed conflicts. (Information, lists and maps of contemporary armed conflicts can be located on the Peace Pledge Union website suggested above or through search engines.)

6 Are there any surprises about the location of conflicts? Are there any surprises about the number of conflicts? Are any of these armed conflicts not reported in the news? Why would conflicts get 'forgotten'?

7 Discuss where pupils had gaps in their knowledge and why that might be. Refer back to the work done on conflict in the news (if appropriate). Discuss how much we learn about conflict and war from the media. How important is it to know about conflicts in the world?

Closing discussion

8 How can we find out more about armed conflicts and wars? Discuss which sources are likely to give: the most factual information; the most interesting; the most up-to-date; the most neutral; the most biased, etc.

9 Pupils should list three things that they have learnt about armed conflict in the world today and give the sources.

Quiz answers

1. 42

Since 1989 – the end of the Cold War between East and West – there have been more than 120 wars worldwide. In the mid-1990s the number of wars increased sharply but the annual total has begun to decrease since the turn of the century.

2. One-third

An average of US$22 billion a year is spent on arms by countries in Africa, Asia, the Middle East and Latin America – a sum that would otherwise enable those countries to be on track to achieve the Millennium Development Goal of achieving universal primary education, as well as targets for reducing infant and maternal mortality. From 1998 to 2001 the USA, the UK and France earned more income from arms sales to developing countries than they gave in aid.

3. Kuwait

The USA is the fifth biggest spender on arms per head of population and the UK is eighth.

4. 56%

Wars today are concentrated in the poorest countries and these countries can very easily get caught up in a cycle of poverty and conflict.

5. 14%

6. 67%

7. 90%

This is the figure since the end of the 'Cold War' in 1989 which marked a change in the types of conflicts waged and how they were financed and fought.

8. Iran

At the end of 2002, around 22 million people across the world were internally displaced – that is, they had to move within their own country to find security. There were 13 million refugees and asylum-seekers seeking protection outside their own countries, most of them women and children.

9. 300,000

It is estimated that roughly 300,000 children under the age of 18 are still participating in armed conflicts around the world. The UK was the last country in Europe to use child soldiers in wars – in 2002 the UK Government agreed to end the deployment of under-18s in military activities as far as possible (although it reserves the right to deploy them if it considers it absolutely neccessary).

10. 8 million

There are approximately 639 million small arms in the world today, produced by more than 1,135 companies in at least 98 countries. Eight million new weapons are produced each year. The proliferation of arms is a major cause of armed conflict and violence. It affects people all over the world, although people in developing countries often suffer disproportionately because controls are not as strict.

Armed conflict quiz

1. Out of approximately 193 countries in the world, how many countries are currently experiencing armed conflict?

    ☐ 21
    ☐ 42
    ☐ 67

2. What proportion of the world's countries spends more on the military than on health-care services?

    ☐ one-fifth (1 in 5)
    ☐ one-third (1 in 3)
    ☐ half (1 in 2)

3. Which country spends the most on arms and weapons per head of population?

    ☐ Israel
    ☐ Kuwait
    ☐ Saudi Arabia

4. Between 1997 and 2001 what percentage of developing countries experienced a civil war?

    ☐ 26%
    ☐ 41%
    ☐ 56%

5. In the First World War, what percentage of casualties were civilians?

    ☐ 14%
    ☐ 67%
    ☐ 90%

6. What percentage of casualties were civilians in the Second World War?

    ☐ 14%
    ☐ 67%
    ☐ 90%

7. What proportion of those killed in conflict since 1989 have been civilians?

    ☐ 14%
    ☐ 67%
    ☐ 90%

8. In 2003 which country in the world had the most refugees?

    ☐ Iran
    ☐ the UK
    ☐ Pakistan

9. How many children are estimated to be involved in conflicts worldwide?

    ☐ 3,000
    ☐ 30,000
    ☐ 300,000

10. How many small arms (guns and other hand-held weapons) are manufactured each year?

    ☐ 3 million
    ☐ 8 million
    ☐ 12 million

(Sources: *United Nations Development Report 2002*, United Nations Children's Fund (UNICEF), United Nations High Commission for Refugees. All statistics relate to 2002 unless otherwise stated.)

Making Sense of World Conflicts

Activity 2.5

Thinking about terrorism

Objectives

- To explore the meanings of 'terrorism'.
- To show that terrorism is a very complex concept.

Learning outcomes

Pupils will have:

- evaluated information
- understood that meaning depends on context.

You will need

- A copy of the poem *My city* on page 33 for each pupil
- A copy of 'Terrorism or fighting for freedom' on page 34 for each pair of pupils
- A copy of 'The rules of war: international humanitarian law' on page 35 for each pair of pupils

Terrorism is an emotive topic and a sensitive one for Muslim children, who have often found themselves on the receiving end of blame and stereotyping since 11 September 2001. Careful pairing and grouping will be important and care will be needed in the discussion on the issues that may be raised. Refer to the section on discussing controversial issues (in the Appendix, page 102) and lay some ground rules for discussion, in particular the avoidance of any racist language or comments.

Starter

1 Give the class the poem *My city* to read to themselves.

2 They should write three words in response to the poem.

3 Pairs should then discuss what they think the poem is about and their reactions to it.

Activity

4 Ask the class for their thoughts on what the poem was about. Did they think it was effective or did they find it moving? Discuss the way in which the poem can be related to either New York or Baghdad, and what that can tell us.

5 If necessary introduce the notion of terrorism. Brainstorm with the class what they think the term 'terrorism' means.

6 Have they heard of the saying 'One person's terrorist is another's freedom fighter'? What does it mean? How and why does the meaning of terrorism depend on the context in which it is used and heard?

7 Give pupils the scenarios on page 34 and ask them to decide whether each of the acts is just or not. If you wish you can introduce the idea of international law and ask pupils to use the resource sheet 'The rules of war: international humanitarian law' to judge the situations.

8 Ask for feedback and discuss their responses.

Closing discussion

9 Where do pupils hear the term 'terrorism' mainly? When did they first become aware of it? What does it make them think of?

10 It is a fact that there is more armed conflict since 11 September 2001 than beforehand. Can there be such a thing as a 'war on terrorism'? Is terrorism an aspect of conflict?

11 Encourage pupils to look and listen out in future for the ways in which the terms 'war' and 'terrorism' are used.

My city

What if life were long
and eternity short?

In my city innocent people
are killed by a thunderous
terror from above. Vendors
in the street are pummeled
by rubble. Men and women
on their way to work are greeted
with the anonymous hatred
of those they have never met.
Janitors, businessmen, clerks,
cooks, construction workers, the rescue
workers who risk all to help these.
My beloved city showered with death.

We cry up and ask, in the midst
of the screams of loved ones,
why do they hate us so?
Why do they do this to our city,
to our lives?
My stomach turns in on itself.
The people I love, burning, dissolving,
dying. The city I love, attacked
from above. My brothers in agony.
My sisters. Children. Mothers. Dead.
Who would do this?
How do we survive this
but by breathing the city's name
over and over like a mantra, a prayer?
Baghdad, Baghdad, Baghdad.

John O'Connor

Terrorism or fighting for freedom?

A   An organisation is trying to get rid of a foreign power from its country. The foreign power controls the country's government and has soldiers in the country. This organisation wants the soldiers to leave and the government to be free to make its own decisions. It goes to the capital city of the foreign power and plants bombs in several popular bars that have a lot of soldiers visiting them. Many civilians and quite a few soldiers die.

B   A leader in a country gains power by rigging an election. To suppress the opposition, the country's army deliberately mistreats people who are against the government: for example, by arresting them and keeping them in prison without charging them with any crime, or by beating them up. The leader of the opposition goes into hiding where he and his followers start a guerrilla war, targeting military installations such as barracks and airbases until they are powerful enough to occupy and keep control of a region of the country. From there they organise a military coup, defeat the country's army and overthrow the government.

C   Two ethnic groups are in dispute over an area of land. One ethnic group has control over this area and curtails the civil liberties of the other. It stops members of the other group from doing certain kinds of jobs (usually well-paid ones) and prevents their children from entering university. It does not let them express their opinions freely without risking being punished. The other group attempts an armed uprising, which is brutally suppressed. Many people are killed or injured. The rebels start to send suicide bombers into crowded civilian areas of the country targeting members of the first ethnic group.

D   A rebel group is trying to make its part of the country into an independent state. It says that its people's language and culture are different from those of the people they are governed by, and they want more control over their own lives. The group organises large demonstrations to show how many people want independence, but nothing happens. Government soldiers shoot people who protest, and destroy their houses. Eventually, members of the rebel group travel to other parts of the country and kidnap civilians. They hold them hostage, demanding that their area becomes independent. Some of these civilians are killed. The group threatens to plant a bomb in a train so that many people will lose their lives.

The rules of war: international humanitarian law

Can acts of war ever be justified? Over the centuries people have thought about this and written books about it. Most people agreed that it was all right for your country to fight back if it was attacked. However, there was some disagreement about whether wars should be fought to resolve other types of dispute.

Now, whether a country may actually use force is governed by a part of international law set out in the United Nations Charter of 1945 which binds nations to live together in peace with one another as good neighbours. Countries are not allowed to use force except:

● in self-defence, or

● when authorised to do so by the United Nations Security Council.

The way a war is fought today is governed by international humanitarian law, which provides a set of rules which seek to limit the effects of armed conflict. A major part of international humanitarian law is found in the Geneva Conventions of 1949, supplemented by the Additional Protocols of 1977 relating to the protection of victims of armed conflicts.

International humanitarian law: the essential rules

The essence of international humanitarian law is summarised below. These rules apply to guerrilla fighters as much as to conventional armies:

● The parties to a conflict must at all times distinguish between civilians and soldiers or fighters in order to spare civilians and their property.

● Attacks may only be made against military targets. Civilians and other people who do not or can no longer take part in the fighting (for example prisoners or wounded soldiers) must not be attacked. 'Terrorist' attacks directed against civilians are thus clearly illegal.

● Armed forces must also take all possible precautions to ensure that they do not kill civilians by accident.

● Neither the parties to the conflict nor members of their armed forces have an unlimited right to choose methods and means of warfare. It is forbidden to use weapons or methods of warfare that are likely to cause unnecessary suffering.

● The wounded and sick must be collected and cared for, no matter which side they fight for. Medical personnel and medical establishments, transport and equipment must not be attacked. The red cross or red crescent on a white background is the distinctive sign which identifies such persons and objects.

● Captured soldiers or fighters and civilians who find themselves under the authority of their enemies must be treated humanely and protected against all acts of violence or revenge. They are entitled to exchange news with their families and receive help.

Further work and sources

These ideas allow further exploration of the nature of conflict and are suitable for projects, assignments, or to be developed into a piece of English coursework.

1 You could ask the class to research definitions of conflict for homework. They could try putting 'definition of conflict' into different search engines and use the online dictionaries that will be accessed. Then create a class display of different definitions.

2 Pupils could try the quiz out on members of their family or others in the school and community. After compiling the answers they could assess the extent of knowledge about present-day armed conflict amongst family or friends. This could lead on to a longer piece of research work or an essay about our understanding of conflict today and the types of gaps in people's knowledge, and some thoughts on consequences for citizenship.

3 Pupils could try making up their own quizzes on aspects of armed conflict, at this and later stages of their work. They could exchange quizzes with other pupils to test increasing knowledge. The quizzes could also be used as part of the research activities outlined above.

4 Pupils could carry out research into how young people react to different types of violence on TV – on the news and in soaps, cartoons and documentaries. This could be done through questionnaires, and the findings compared with research findings that can be accessed on the web: for example, the Community Learning Network (an American site) **www.cln.org** – click on 'Theme pages' and then 'Violence in the media'; and Media Awareness Network (a Canadian site) **www.media-awareness.ca** – click on 'Media issues'. Pupils could then write an essay summarising the findings and putting forward their own point of view.

5 Pupils could carry out a survey of the language used in the news when reporting conflict. A link to 'Peace journalism' (see Chapter 7) could be made.

6 Pupils could debate or write essays on moral dilemmas to do with conflict, such as 'Is it a terrorist act to assassinate a dictator such as Hitler?'

7 Pupils could consider some recent wars, such as the war in Iraq, in the light of international humanitarian law (see page 35) and debate whether the war was justified.

8 Pupils could research organisations which have been called both terrorists and freedom fighters such as the ANC, the Zapatistas and the Turkish PKK. They could try to present balanced arguments and then put forward their own point of view.

9 Suggest creative writing:
   ● around one or more of the images in the chapter
   ● around one of the proverbs
   ● in response to the poem *My city* and the work on terrorism.

10 Read some of Aesop's fables and discuss the responses to conflict within the tales.

11 Collect cartoons relating to conflict from newspapers and magazines, and make a display including comments and questions.

Developing skills of enquiry and evaluating information

Aims for this chapter:

- To present a variety of non-fiction material relating to causes of conflict, using the genocide in Rwanda as a case study to explore social and moral issues.
- To enable pupils to develop skills of enquiry, critical analysis and evaluation of media and non-fiction texts.

The case study

This chapter looks at causes of conflict, and in particular ways to investigate and understand causes of national and international conflicts. It uses the conflict and genocide in Rwanda as a case study. This case study has been chosen for a number of reasons:

- It is in the past (1994) with the advantage of the perspective which time brings to events, but there has been continuing interest in examining the causes, especially when the ten-year anniversary took place.
- It is a conflict which pupils may have heard referred to but may not know much about.
- It is important that pupils do know something of this conflict, as it is the worst case of genocide within recent history and is often quoted as an example of the type of conflict that must never be allowed to happen again.
- It is a difficult conflict to talk about and teach as there were terrible atrocities. The images and stories coming from the region at the time and later were extremely disturbing and so this particular example of conflict will often be avoided.
- This material and these approaches are offered as examples of ways to deal with controversial and difficult conflict issues in the classroom.

The skills, knowledge and understanding developed through the case study can be applied to other conflict situations and events. Important skills are those of questioning, investigating, analysing and debating. Important approaches are those of looking at different viewpoints and perspectives, recognising that causes are complex and interlinked and that there is no definitive understanding of how a conflict was caused.

Activities in this chapter:

- Introductory activity: conflict scenarios
- Why did it happen? Enquiring and analysing
- Why did it happen? Viewpoints and the media

Activities 5.1 and 5.2, which are concerned with the effects of conflict on people's lives, also feature source material on Rwanda.

Activity 3.1

Introductory activity: conflict scenarios

Introduce this activity as a way of beginning to explore different causes of conflict in a familiar setting. This is in preparation for investigating and analysing the ways in which causes of conflict in the wider world can be accessed and understood. It can be used to compare with how causes of conflict are reported and explained in the media.

Objectives

- To introduce conflict as an issue to explore through drama activities.
- To reflect on experiences of the causes of conflict.

Learning outcomes

Pupils will have:

- used different dramatic techniques to explore causes of everyday conflicts
- used their imagination to consider other people's experiences.

You will need

- A copy of one of the 'Conflict scenarios' on page 39 for each group

Starter

1   As a class discuss briefly what is meant by 'a cause' and 'an effect'.
2   Pairs of pupils could come up with a simple example – the effect of the bath overflowing was that the floor was flooded; the cause was that the taps were left running too long.

Activity

3   Divide the class into pairs or small groups and give each one a 'Conflict scenario' (copy and cut up page 39). Ask them to discuss the questions at the end.
4   Ask for feedback and discuss the different responses.
5   Then carry out speaking and listening drama activities. Divide the class into different groups and ask them to improvise short dramas based on their scenario. They should include some development of the situation. Choose one or more groups to act their scenario in front of the class. After the drama ask the characters to remain in role and answer questions from the class about their motives and their feelings.
6   Discuss with the whole class the way in which the scenarios were developed. Did the situation become a conflict? If so, why? What were the causes? Was there more than one? Which was the most significant cause? Was conflict inevitable or could it have been avoided?

Closing discussion

7   Pupils can discuss and identify one possible cause of conflict at each level – personal, community, national, international, global. Are the causes – such as beliefs, possessions or control of power – similar at each level ?

Conflict scenarios

A You and your friends from school sometimes go to the local café after school and sit at the table in the window. One day there are some kids from another school hanging about outside. When you approach they start making loud comments about you and your school. They go in just before you and sit at the window table. You all sit at another table but the other kids continue to look over at you and make comments under their breath.

How do you feel? What happens when your group leaves the café?

B One day the teacher says that all pupils who have completed their coursework will be able to work on the computers with access to a special revision lesson. All the other pupils in the class must sit silently and revise on their own. The teacher will be available to help those on the computers. Anyone revising silently who talks will get a detention.

Which group would you be in? How do you feel? What happens afterwards?

C Your friend has been very unhappy recently. You find out that your friend gets bullied by members of a local gang who make racist comments. You discuss what to do and eventually you convince your friend to tell your Head of Year. You both like and respect the Head of Year who is fair and effective and has always encouraged those with difficulties to come forward. But the trouble continues and nothing seems to happen, even though the teacher promised to sort it out.

How does your friend feel? How do you feel? What happens in a few weeks time?

D Your brother goes to a different school. He is always going on about how much better it is than your school and how they have better facilities and teachers. You get fed up with this because you think your school is fine. But then you read in the local paper that your brother's school is getting some extra money from the government to build a new library and sports hall and there will be laptop computers in all the classrooms. Your school doesn't seem to be getting anything.

How do you feel? What happens when you talk to your mates in school about this?

E In Citizenship you have been talking about democracy and how everyone has the right to express their views and have their opinions taken into account. You think it would be a good idea to set up a school council so that pupils' ideas and views about school life can be discussed. You talk to everyone in your form and get their backing and then you put the idea to your teacher who supports you. The school council gets going but it turns out that you are only allowed to discuss certain things – the insignificant things. Discussing teachers or teaching is not allowed.

How do you feel? What happens next?

Making Sense of World Conflicts

Activity 3.2

Why did it happen? Enquiring and analysing

Objectives

- To understand some reasons why conflict takes place.

Learning outcomes

Pupils will have:

- developed skills of enquiry and analysis
- selected, compared and synthesised information from different texts.

You will need

- A copy of the poem and the causes of conflict on page 41 for each pupil

Starter

1 Put on the board 'things', 'feelings' and 'ideas'.

2 Brainstorm conflicts (not necessarily armed conflicts) that pupils may be aware of – locally, nationally or internationally. These could range from a local dispute about a new road to a war between countries or the 'war on terror'.

3 Ask pupils to attempt to decide fairly quickly whether the conflicts are about things, feelings or ideas, or a combination.

4 Briefly discuss this task and its difficulty.

Activity

5 Ask pupils in groups to read the poem, *The people of the other village*, and discuss what it is about.

6 Ask for feedback. Is the poem about causes of conflict or its effects or both? Can pupils relate any causes of conflict suggested in the poem to the three very general causes of conflict – things, feelings and ideas?

7 The poem is written by an American, Thomas Lux, who was born in Massachusetts in 1946. Why might he have written the poem? Could the poem relate to conflict anywhere?

8 For an English lesson you could go on to discuss conflict that features in literature that the class have studied. Discuss whether the conflict relates to things, feelings or ideas.

9 For a Humanities lesson discuss with pupils the list of causes of conflict at national and international level. There are some difficult concepts here which may need explaining. Relate these causes to some examples if possible.

10 In their groups pupils should choose one conflict that they are reasonably familiar with (they could choose one from literature or a historical conflict that they have studied). Explain that you would now like them to create their own 'concept map' to summarise the causes of their chosen conflict on a large sheet of paper. They can use any representations they like – words, drawings, symbols – and should try to make links between the causes where possible.

11 Ask each group to present their diagram to the rest of the class, explaining any links between the causes and their reasons for making them.

Closing discussion

12 Refer back to the poem *The people of the other village* and discuss its message.

The people of the other village

hate the people of this village
and would nail our hats
to our heads for refusing in their presence to remove them
or staple our hands to our foreheads
for refusing to salute them
if we did not hurt them first: mail them packages of rats,
mix their flour at night with broken glass.
We do this, they do that.
They peel the larynx from one of our brothers' throats.
We devein one of their sisters.
The quicksand pits they built were good.
Our amputation teams were better.
We trained some birds to steal their wheat.
They sent to us exploding ambassadors of peace.
They do this, we do that.
We canceled our sheep imports.
They no longer bought our blankets.
We mocked their greatest poet
and when that had no effect
we parodied the way they dance
which did cause pain, so they, in turn, said our God
was leprous, hairless.
We do this, they do that.
Ten thousand (10,000) years, ten thousand
(10,000) brutal, beautiful years.

Thomas Lux (born Massachusetts, USA, 1946)

The causes of conflict

The causes of conflict in general ...
● Conflicts over things
● Conflicts over feelings
● Conflicts over ideas

... and at national and international level
● Colonialism
● Ethnic division
● Disputed land or border
● Outside interference
● Religious division
● Lack of democracy
● Political ideology
● Lack of access to resources
● Poverty

Activity 3.3

Why did it happen? Viewpoints and the media

Objectives

- To understand some of the complexity of the reasons for the conflict in Rwanda.
- To recognise the significance of the media in society.

Learning outcomes

Pupils will have:

- compared and synthesised information from different texts.
- expressed and justified opinions orally.

You will need

For part one:

- 'Rwanda: country profile' on page 44, a copy for each pair
- 'Rwanda: what happened and why?' copies of Source A on page 45 for half the class and Source B on page 46 for the other half

For part two:

- 'Looking back: points of view' on page 47, a copy for each pair
- 'Looking back: the power of the media' on page 48, a copy for each pair

This activity will take longer than one lesson and is presented in two parts so that it can be run as a sequence of lessons.

Explain that this activity uses the conflict and genocide in Rwanda in 1994 as a case study. Pupils will be investigating views of the causes of conflict. Sensitivity will be required if there are children whose families may have been affected by conflict in Central Africa, and also because details of the events are extremely shocking. It is important to remember, however, that genocide can happen anywhere in the world, not only in poor countries.

Starter

1   Locate Rwanda in Africa on a map or globe with the class. Ask the class if they have heard of the 1994 conflict in Rwanda. Hand out copies of the 'country profile' on page 44 and ask pupils to read it and list three things they have learnt about Rwanda.

Activity – Part one

2   Working in groups, half the class should read Source A and the other half should read Source B of 'Rwanda: what happened and why?' on pages 45–46. Ask each group to note or underline three causes of the conflict in Rwanda that are mentioned.

3   Ask Source A groups to report back and note the causes on the board, then ask for feedback from Source B groups and note the causes on the board in a separate list. Are the lists the same or different? Why might this be? (Keep the lists for later.)

4   Discuss the styles in which the pieces are written and the purpose of each piece. Points could include that Source A is a factual piece but includes some emotive vocabulary such as 'unleashing', 'sanctuary' and 'grinding' to underline the horror of the situation. It could be written for people in the UK who might want to help reduce poverty in African countries as it underlines the struggle of the Rwandan people for a better life and comes from Oxfam. Source B is more opinionated and is a personal assessment of the causes by an African from a nearby country, probably a historian. It is likely to have been written for people who would be interested in an African point of view.

5   Talk with pupils about any questions that may be raised by looking at these pieces. They may wish to find out more about the conflict before the next lesson.

Activity – Part two

6   Recap the causes of the conflict in Rwanda discussed in the previous lesson. Give each pair a copy of the quotations from the press on page 47, which appeared at the time of the ten-year anniversary of the conflict. They should underline causes that are mentioned. Compare the causes mentioned with those listed in the previous lesson. Are they different? Are there contradictions? What is meant by 'hindsight'?

7   Ask pupils to work in pairs and give each pair a copy of the headlines on page 48. The headlines are a sample of those that appeared at the beginning of April 2004 and represent the balance of types of headlines at the time.

8   Some of the headlines are from the UK press and some are from the press in different African countries. Ask pairs of pupils to decide which are which, with reasons for their choices. And ask them to underline key words in the headlines.

9   Take feedback and then tell them where each headline comes from (see page 43). Were there any surprises? Why? Which keywords are positive and which negative or neutral? Overall, do the media send out an optimistic or pessimistic message about Rwanda's future by their use of language in the headlines? How might this affect readers of newspapers?

10 Why was the anniversary considered to be news? Why would the media want to report and comment on the anniversary and what happened in the past? What role did the media appear to take on at the time of the anniversary?

Glossary

Genocide The deliberate killing of an ethnic, religious, political or national group. Genocide is defined in the Genocide Convention of 1948 as acts 'committed with intent to destroy, in whole or in part, a national, ethnical, racial or religious group'. It is this deliberate attempt to exterminate a group which distinguishes it from other forms of conflict. The Genocide Convention puts an obligation on signatory states to intervene to prevent genocide, and to punish its perpetrators.

11 Discuss the role that the media appear to have played in Rwanda at the time of the conflict. What do the short extracts on page 48 say about the power of the media?

Closing discussion

12 What can be learnt about identifying causes of the conflict in Rwanda? Does it seem likely that there will usually be many and complex causes of conflicts around the world? Can pupils suggest examples of conflicts where there are many and complex causes?

Sources of headlines from 'Looking back: the power of the media'

Headlines from UK press, March/April 2004 sourced from:
A (*Daily Telegraph*); C, F, G (*The Guardian*); J, L (*The Independent*).

Headlines from African press March/April 2004 sourced from **http://allafrica.com**:
B (*Ghanaian Chronicle*); D (*New Vision*); E, H (*East African*); I,K (*East African Standard*).

Rwandan President Paul Kagame arriving at a sports field near Nyagatare, where he was to give a speech ▶

Ami Vitale / Oxfam

Ami Vitale / Oxfam

◀ Crowned cranes at Lake Muhazi, eastern Rwanda. Known as the 'land of a thousand hills', Rwanda is famous for its mountains, lakes and wildlife. The government is working to rebuild the tourist industry.

Rwanda: country profile

The country has been beset by ethnic tension associated with the traditionally unequal relationship between the dominant Tutsi minority and the majority Hutus. Rwanda experienced Africa's worst genocide in modern times in 1994 and is still recovering from the effects. Many people had to flee to neighbouring countries to escape the killing.

Since then, most of the refugees have returned to Rwanda. In 2000 Paul Kagame became President of Rwanda under an interim government. His government soon introduced a policy encouraging people to describe themselves as Rwandans rather than Hutus or Tutsis. His presidency was confirmed in a landslide victory in the 2003 election.

The country continues to work to boost investment and agricultural output and to foster reconciliation, but involvement in two wars over the past eight years in the neighbouring Democratic Republic of Congo has hindered its efforts.

Population:
7.954 million

Capital: Kigali

Major religions:
Christianity, indigenous beliefs

Ethnic groups:
Hutu 84%, Tutsi 15%, Twa 1%

Life expectancy:
39 years (men), 40 years (women)

Main exports:
Coffee, tea, hides, tin ore

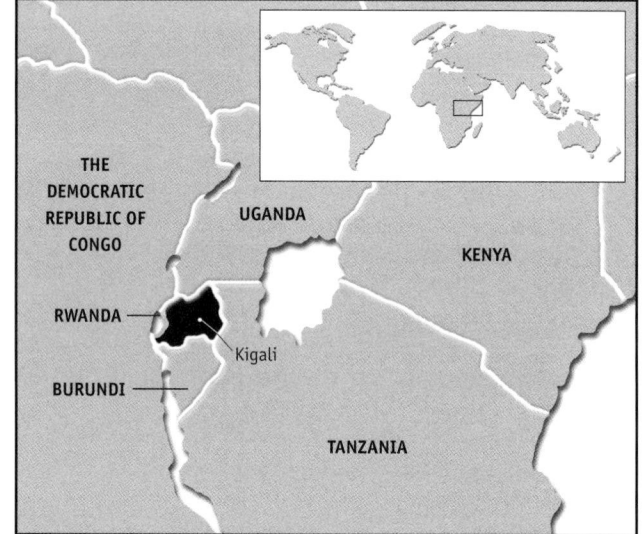

Media: Rwanda's broadcast media are, in the main, government-controlled. A privately run radio station, the first to open since the 1994 genocide, began broadcasting in 2004.

There is a growing number of newspapers but they face government restrictions and generally exercise self-censorship.

Climate: Temperate; two rainy seasons (February to April, November to January); mild in mountains with frost and snow possible.

Physical features: Rwanda is a beautiful country. The forest-covered mountains in the west give way to fertile, terraced farmland, tea plantations and rolling hills, before turning into savannah in the east. The Virunga mountains in the northwest along the border with the Democratic Republic of Congo are the home of the only surviving mountain gorilla population in the world.

Rwanda: what happened and why?

SOURCE A

What happened in Rwanda in 1994?

Between April and July 1994 an estimated 800,000 people, mainly from Rwanda's minority Tutsi ethnic group, were killed in a systematic campaign orchestrated by extremist elements of the country's majority Hutu ethnic group. The dead also included politically moderate Hutu. The killings were long planned but sparked by the shooting down on 6 April 1994 of a plane carrying Rwanda's Hutu president, Juvenal Habyarimana and his Burundian counterpart.

This was the catalyst for the unleashing of a well-planned campaign of genocide by Rwanda's extremist 'Hutu Power' movement. Supported by extensive radio hate propaganda, militias known as *Interahamwe* ('those who work together') spearheaded a programme of massacres, largely carried out with machetes, but sometimes also using modern small arms to force people together before the killing. Victims were hacked to death, burnt alive, thrown dead or alive into pits or latrines, forced to murder their own friends or relatives. At least 250,000 Tutsi women and girls were raped, many of them by HIV-positive men who wanted to spread Aids.

In just 100 days, Rwanda's population was decimated: of an original population of about seven and a half million, at least 800,000 people were killed. About two million Rwandans became refugees and sought sanctuary in camps in the former Zaire (now the Democratic Republic of Congo) and other countries. Many of these people also perished from diseases such as cholera and other causes.

What is the historical background and what caused the genocide?

Historical tensions between the Hutu and Tutsi groups had been worsened by the policies of Rwanda's colonial rulers – Germany from the 1890s, then Belgium from the First World War. Both reinforced the Tutsis' position of power within Rwandan society, increasing Hutu resentments. Rwanda was Africa's most densely populated nation; 90 per cent of its people are subsistence farmers and competition for land is intense. The majority of the population were non-literate and living in grinding poverty.

When the Hutu majority finally gained power after independence in 1962, many Tutsi fled to neighbouring countries such as Uganda, Zaire (now the Democratic Republic of Congo) and Burundi. An army of Tutsi exiles called the Rwandan Patriotic Front (RPF) formed in Uganda in 1979 and invaded Rwanda in 1990, sparking a civil war.

In August 1993, the international community backed a power-sharing peace deal between the Rwandan government and the RPF. But the warning signs of imminent violence against the Tutsi were increasing. With a concerted propaganda campaign, the Hutu Power movement was able to play on land hunger, lack of education and historical resentment to instil hatred for all Tutsi.

(Source: www.oxfam.org.uk)

Rwanda: what happened and why?

SOURCE B

Reasons for the Rwandan genocide

Julian Cobbing, Professor of History at Rhodes University suggests reasons for the genocide. These, he says, include the question of over-population and consequently pressure on land and its resources as less land became available for cultivation and more people ran out of food. Cobbing cites another reason as the ethnic rivalry between the Tutsis and the Hutus fomented by the Belgians as part of the colonial rule policy of divide and rule. He maintains that the differences between the Hutus and the Tutsis were a lie because they speak the same language and it is impossible to tell their differences.

Cobbing locates the emergence of the Rwandan genocide on the assumption of power by the Hutus in 1962 under President Juvenal Habyarimana. Owing to the collapse of the world coffee prices in the late 1980s, the government accumulated a huge foreign debt that was difficult for it to service and started to run out of money.

By 1992, Rwanda faced incursions from the rebels of the Rwandan Patriotic Front led by Rwandan Tutsi refugees. At the same time, the devaluation of the local currency, rocketing food prices, massive inflation and unemployment meant life generally became difficult for most Rwandans around this time and they began to resent the Hutu-led government.

The Hutu elite organised youth militias dubbed the *Interahamwe* to augment the power of the 40,000-plus Rwandan army, while the French sent money and weapons. By 1991–93, the situation had worsened for the political elite who were increasingly surrounded by not-so-friendly African countries pressing for political reforms, democracy and elections, but the elite was not prepared to abandon power. They found the solution in the elimination of Tutsis, and the only way out was for them to be removed from power by force.

In April 1994 President Habyarimana's plane was shot down outside Kigali killing everyone on board. No one knew who was responsible, with some saying it was the Hutu extremists while others blamed the Tutsis. Within two hours of the shooting down of the plane, the genocide ensued and it took a week for it to spread across the country. Ordinary people, who included peasants and neighbours in villages, joined in obeying elite orders to kill their neighbours from 'the other tribe'.

(Source: Based on an article by Donny Dithato, *Mmegi/The Reporter* (Gaborone), 7 April 2004 http://allafrica.com)

Looking back: points of view

The finger of accusation

In a speech during the commemoration of this unfathomable crime against humanity, the current President of Rwanda, Paul Kagame, pointed a strong finger of accusation against the international community for its well-documented failure to intervene to avert the tragedy.

Kagame deplored the 'blatant indifference' of the international community, adding that wherever genocide occurred in the world it represents the failure of the developed countries to act.

(Source: *Financial Gazette* (Harare), 8 April 2004
http://allafrica.com)

Taking responsibility

President Paul Kagame of Rwanda said during his speech at Amahoro Stadium in Kigali, where one of the biggest events of the commemoration of the tenth anniversary of the genocide is taking place: 'Even though the seed of the genocide was from the colonial government, they were bystanders. Rwandans should take the primary responsibility for what happened ten years ago.'

(Source: *Hirondelle News Agency* (Lausanne), 7 April 7 2004
http://allafrica.com)

Not paying enough attention

Ten years following one of the world's most gruesome mass murders in the East African state of Rwanda, the United Nations has once again shared [sic]blame on herself and other international actors operating in that country at the time. The day was commemorated worldwide on Wednesday... The Secretary General's message recalled that the Rwanda genocide should never have happened, but it did because neither the UN Secretariat, nor the Security Council, including the member states in general, and the international media, paid enough attention to the gathering signs of the disaster.

(Source: Stanley Mcgill, *The News* (Monrovia), 8 April 2004
http://allafrica.com)

Learning the lessons

The racist argument that Rwanda is an ill-educated and primitive society does not wash. Both Germans and Serbians were advanced and apparently civilised people, yet from their midst there stepped forward large numbers of individuals prepared to perpetrate these enormities ... But there is one lesson that can be learned by all decent people who recoil at such cruelty. It is that history has shown time and again that the outside world has stood by for far too long before intervening in these ethnic bloodbaths.

(Source: *Arab News*, Saudi Arabia, 7 April 2004
www.guardian.co.uk)

Looking back: the power of the media

Headlines from African and UK newspapers in March/April 2004 at the time of the tenth anniversary of the genocide in Rwanda.

A)   How the West turned blind eye despite general's 'genocide fax'

B)   Rwanda, 10 years later: could it happen in Ghana?

C)   Rwanda: peace but no reconciliation

D)   United Nations mst do more to stop bloodbaths

E)   Blame France, learn nothing from Rwanda

F)   'The UN let people die and now it watches as the survivors die'

G)   US chose to ignore Rwandan genocide

H)   Accusations and tears as East Africa remembers 1994

I)   Renewed hope as recovery path is paved

J)   Digging deep: the British brothers who are building hope in Rwanda

K)   Kagame set genocide in motion, Paris judge says

L)   Sudan is another Rwanda in the making

The influence of the Rwandan media

Broadcaster jailed for inciting genocide

The International Criminal Tribunal for Rwanda sentenced Ruggiu, 42, on two counts of directly and publicly inciting people to commit genocide in his broadcasts for Radio Télévision Libre des Mille Collines in Rwanda... Amnesty International's UK director, Kate Allen, said: 'Rwandese radio was a powerful tool for spreading genocidal hate and today's sentence demonstrates the international community's determination to send out its own message that systematic killing will not go unpunished.'

(Source: Ian Black in Brussels and Ewen MacAskill, *The Guardian*, 2 June 2000)

Poison pens

John Floyd [American counsel for Hassan Ngeze who edited a newspaper *Kangura* – meaning Awakening – a vehicle for virulent anti-Tutsi propaganda] says the prosecutions would not have been brought in the US... 'What's on trial here is free speech and the freedom of the press... We're talking about a judgement which, potentially, will be used to justify censorship.'

(Source: Jon Silverman, *The Guardian*, 24 June 2002)

Mounting incitement

During the 1994 genocide ... one announcer promised that this war would 'exterminate the Tutsi from the globe'... Andrew Puddephatt, of Article 19, the London based anti-censorship organisation, said: 'Freedom of expression is a fundamental human right, but not unlimited. It has to be balanced against respect for other human rights.'

(Source: Mark Thompson, *The Guardian*, 26 August 2002)

Further work and sources

These ideas allow further exploration of the causes of conflict and are suitable for projects, assignments, or to be developed into a piece of English coursework.

1   Discuss a local conflict that pupils are aware of. You may be able to provide local newspaper articles or recorded radio and TV coverage. Alternatively they could research material and perhaps carry out interviews. Can they work out the causes of the conflict and relate them to generic causes (e.g. ethnic division, lack of access to resources, outside interference)? They could then either choose to present their own views, backed up by reasoned argument and relevant audio-visual material, or write and present a script for a short local TV news piece about the conflict.

2   Pupils could choose a conflict being reported in the news and aim to investigate the causes of the conflict. They should aim to analyse and understand some of the complexities. Initially they will need to carry out research and can access information from press and media websites (see Resources section on page 108–110), or collect information from newspapers and TV on a daily basis.

    As part of their investigation they could evaluate sources of information on the conflict and consider how easy it is to find out about the causes from the daily news reports and other sources. Which sources do they think are the most informative and why?

3   If pupils have become interested in finding out more about Rwanda and the other countries in the region that were involved in conflict, such as Burundi, they could carry out research into the country and the region, its people and its history. The aim of the research could be to create a presentation to give to the rest of the class, or a series of posters or exhibition boards for display. Encourage pupils to look at websites and information from a range of countries and organisations, such as Rwandan community associations in the UK, to get different perspectives. Pupils should be encouraged to carry out critical analysis of the websites that they use, looking at use of images and language, who is providing information and who is given a voice.

4   Pupils could consider the texts they have been reading and working on in class and look for examples of conflict. They could construct a series of key questions for an investigation, such as:
    ● Where does conflict occur?
    ● How is it presented?
    ● What are the causes of this conflict, specifically and generically?
    ● Are the causes explicit or implicit?
    ● Can any useful comparisons be made?
    ● Are there any texts where conflict does not appear, and why?

    References should be made to the texts. An extended piece of writing can be planned and carried out.

5   You might want to consider the issues of the right of free speech versus the need to prevent genocide (cf. the role of the media in the Rwandan genocide) and ask pupils to write an essay on this or prepare cases for a debate.

Discussing a topical issue, arguing a case

Aims for this chapter:

- To introduce the challenging issue of gun culture and examine reactions in the light of information about the realities of violence.
- To make the connections between local gun cultures and the global arms trade.
- To enable pupils to develop skills of enquiry, critical analysis and evaluation of media and non-fiction texts relating to gun culture and the arms trade.

The case studies

This chapter uses case studies from Brazil and the UK. Its focus is on the devastating results of armed conflict and the arms trade, gun culture and violence in communities. There are many initiatives around the world where people and communities are working together to reduce violence, control arms in communities and educate young people to reject gun culture. Initiatives for change that relate to the case studies in Brazil and the UK are included in the source material in Chapter 7 and you might like to make sure that pupils are aware that there is positive action being taken.

Activities in this chapter:

- The increasing use of small arms: putting over a message
- The arms bazaar – a mystery
- The human cost of arms abuse – the real deal
- Role play: public inquiry

Activity 4.1

The increasing use of small arms: putting over a message

Objectives

- To recognise how the use of images and words can convey powerful messages.
- To create a basis of understanding of the issues of small arms and the arms trade.

Learning outcomes

Pupils will have:

- identified some initial facts about the increasing use of small arms
- analysed how words can work with pictures to create meaning.

You will need

- A copy of 'The increasing use of small arms' on page 52, for each pair
- You could also use the Control Arms campaign source material on page 96 in Chapter 7

Glossary

Small arms Small arms are designed for personal use; light weapons are designed for use by several people serving as a crew. Small arms include revolvers and self-loading pistols; rifles and carbines; sub-machine guns; assault rifles; and light machine guns.

Starter

1   Inform pupils of the meaning of 'small arms'. Give pairs of pupils a copy of the statements on page 52 and ask them to try to decide whether each is true or false. They should mark each statement with a T or an F. Go through the answers – all the statements are true! The statements are hard-hitting, so ask pupils which they find the most surprising and which the most shocking and why.

Activity

2   Ask pupils to look at the image on page 52, which is a campaign poster aimed at children in Cambodia designed to raise awareness of the danger of playing with old munitions. Enlarge on a photocopier if necessary. Do not give any information at this stage.

3   Ask the pupils what they think this picture is about? What does it show? What might it be for? Who might it be aimed at? What part of the world might it come from? How might we know? Discuss the visual clues to the message and meaning of the image. Then give the pupils information about the poster. Note that the picture shows an unexploded bomb, which is not really a small arm. However, the issues are the same: there are too many being manufactured, and they are falling into the wrong hands.

4   Ask pupils to choose one or more of the statements that best relates to the poster, or to make up their own caption. Do the words increase the power of the message? How?

5   You might like to discuss the posters designed by the Saatchi Advertising Agency on the dangers of landmines in Cambodia. Visit the website of the International Campaign to Ban Landmines at **www.icbl.org**, click on 'Tools' and then click on 'Image Library' and search on Saatchi. There is plenty of other visual material there as well.

6   You could also provide some information about the legacy of small arms use in Cambodia which can be found by using the search option on the Oxfam website **www.oxfam.org.uk** and the Control Arms campaign website **www.controlarms.org**, or by using a search engine.

Closing discussion

7   Do people in the UK have to worry about the dangers of small arms and discarded weapons? Discuss how it would affect our lives if there were a significant risk from discarded small arms and weapons. What three points would pupils use to warn people of the dangers of small arms? Pupils could design a poster for homework based on one of the statements about the increasing use of small arms.

The increasing use of small arms

A. Small arms kill more people than weapons of mass destruction.

B. Small arms are present in every country in the world.

C. Small arms are the only weapons used in most conflicts.

D. Nine out of ten atrocities committed against civilians involve the use of small arms.

E. The availability of small arms increases the risk of death and injury.

F. Injury rates are likely to rise once a war is over.

G. Domestic violence is now more likely to occur and end in serious injury.

H. Small arms are lighter than ever before.

I. Small arms are cheaper than ever before.

J. There are 639 million small arms in the world, or one for every ten people.

K. Small arms are produced by over 1,000 companies, in at least 98 countries.

L. Eight million more small arms are produced every year.

M. Sixteen billion units of ammunition are produced every year.

N. Nearly 60 per cent of small arms are in civilian hands.

(Source: A to I from Oxfam publications, J to N from www.oxfam.org.uk)

Howard Davies / Oxfam

Activity 4.2

The arms bazaar: a mystery

Objectives

- To interpret information and make judgements informed by reasons and evidence.

- To create a basis of understanding of the issues of arms dealing and the arms trade.

Learning outcomes

Pupils will have:

- identified some initial facts about the increasing use of small arms

- used information sorting, processing, interpreting and explaining skills.

You will need

- 'Statements: the arms bazaar' on pages 54–55, with the statements cut up in envelopes for each group of three pupils. For teachers who wish to differentiate, a shorter and simpler version of this exercise can be made by missing out statements 18 to 25 inclusive

- A copy of 'The increasing use of small arms' on page 52, for each pair (opitional)

> *The Georgian soldiers used to give bullets to kids to play with, and if you gave them some vodka or cigarettes, they'd give you anything – a small gun or a grenade.*

Georgi, 14 years old, originally from Abkhazia in Georgia, but now displaced, 2000

You will need to have discussed the meaning of small arms. You will find a definition in the Glossary on page 106.

Starter

1   In pairs, pupils should complete the following sentences

- 'If I ruled the school, my rule on weapons would be ...'
- 'If I ruled my family, my rule on weapons would be ...'
- 'If I ruled the community, my rule on weapons would be ...'
- 'If I ruled the country, my rule on weapons would be ...'
- 'If I ruled the world, my rule on weapons would be ...'

2   Ask for brief feedback and discuss the similarities in the lists.

Activity

3   This is a 'thinking skills' activity. Pupils will carry out a 'mystery' exercise in which they are given 25 statements on individual pieces of paper and should produce an answer to a central question. The question is: **Why is there a big increase in the number of arms in the world?** The mystery is designed to encourage pupils to deal with ambiguity through addressing a question which has no single correct answer and where they are not even sure what information is relevant, so they must sift and evaluate ideas. It is important that the statements are presented on separate pieces of paper so that pupils can physically categorise them and move them around. The successful completion of the task depends on co-operative group work – three in a group is recommended.

4   Give each group an envelope with the cut-up statements from pages 54–55 inside and the key question that they must answer written on the envelope. You can also give them copies of the 'The increasing use of small arms' statements as supporting material if you wish. Ask groups to lay out all the statements in any order and check if there are any words that need explaining.

5   Explain that they are going to become detectives and use the statements to come up with an answer to the key question. There is not a right order or a right answer. Tell them that sorting the statements is important but they need to keep looking at the links between statements. As detectives they must come up with the most convincing explanation using the evidence plus any other knowledge of the issue. They should give as much detail as they can.

6   You might need to think about how to ask pupils to give their feedback, as lower-ability groups will need more structure. They could, for example, be asked to identify five key answers to the question (giving evidence) and then rank them. As groups work, check that they are manipulating the information effectively and give guidance if necessary.

7   Ask each group to report back to the class on their answer to the mystery, giving their reasons. Discuss the findings.

Closing discussion

8   Ask for feedback on the activity and discuss the responses. Discuss with the class anything that surprised them about the information on the arms trade or arms companies. What do they think could or should be done about the situation?

Statements: the arms bazaar

1. The UK is the world's second-largest arms exporting country.

2. Small arms have been used in both Sierra Leone and Liberia to kill and maim many innocent civilians, yet nobody involved in supplying any of these arms has been prosecuted or held accountable for their actions.

3. In March 1999, a Ukrainian arms broker, Leonid Minin, was responsible for delivering weapons, including 2,000 AK-47 assault rifles, 50 machine guns, ammunition, rocket-propelled grenades, anti-tank weapons and surface-to-air missiles, from Ukraine to Liberia and to rebel forces in Sierra Leone.

4. In 2001 China, France, the Russian Federation, the UK and the USA were the top five arms exporters in the world, together responsible for 88 per cent of arms exports.

5. Illegal arms deals involve a complex web of front companies, false or misleading paperwork, transport and different trails originating from many different countries.

6. MBDA (a UK-owned arms company), produces some of the world's most advanced future missile systems and its ambition is to offer customers the best and most cost-efficient solutions and services for their defence requirements in missiles and missile systems.

7. Arms can travel around the world and reach conflict zones and countries with poor human rights records or high levels of organised crime.

8. Between 1960 and 1999, the number of countries producing small arms doubled and there was an almost six-fold increase in the number of companies manufacturing them.

9. Nearly 60 per cent of small arms are in civilian hands.

10. Leonid Minin's arms deals were made possible by companies and individuals based in countries as diverse as Gibraltar, the UK, Burkina Faso, Côte D'Ivoire and the Ukraine.

11. The control of arms trading is left to individual governments, who may be unwilling or unable to ensure responsible practices.

12. DRS Technologies (a US-owned arms company) states that it is a defence technology leader and provides leading-edge products and services to defence, government, intelligence and commercial customers.

Statements: the arms bazaar

13. Between 1998 and 2002 there was an 11-fold increase in the number of components licensed for sale in the UK.

14. Italian police arrested Leonid Minin near Milan on 5 August 2000. When police raided his hotel, documents relating to questionable arms deals were found in his possession.

15. In March 1999, any arms deals to Sierra Leone and Liberia were illegal and outlawed by the United Nations.

16. China, France, the Russian Federation, the UK and the USA are heavily involved in the business of arms trading and profiting from it.

17. Leonid Minin walked free from prosecution when Italian authorities decided they could not prosecute him under Italian law because the arms he supplied, although outlawed by the United Nations, had never passed over Italian soil.

18. The majority of weapons used in conflict situations are not produced by the countries involved.

19. BAe Systems (a UK-owned arms company) states that it is a systems company innovating for a safer world and is a company with vision and values.

20. The USA dominates the arms industry, contributing almost half (45 per cent) of all the world's exported weapons.

21. Recent research has identified 1,135 companies manufacturing small arms and ammunition in at least 98 countries; these numbers are increasing all the time.

22. From 1998 to 2001, the USA, the UK, and France earned more income from arms sales to developing countries than they gave in aid.

23. One of the key features of the trade in arms is the way that weapons pass from the legal sector into the illegal sphere. The boundary between the two is extremely weak.

24. There is an increasing trade in components (parts that are used to make small arms and weapons) which are more likely to be given licences for trade with fewer controls.

25. DRS Technologies (US-owned arms company) develops and manufactures a broad range of mission critical systems, which are sold to all branches of the US military, government agencies, major aerospace and defence contractors, and international military forces.

Activity 4.3

The human cost of arms abuse: the real deal

Objectives

- To consider the impact of arms abuse on people's lives.
- To critique the ways in which conflict and arms can represent something to be admired and desired.

Learning outcomes

Pupils will have:

- formed their own view, taking into account a range of evidence and opinions
- developed their evaluation skills.

You will need

- A copy of the UK case study 'Gangs and guns: who takes the rap?' on page 57, for each pair
- A copy of the Brazil case study 'Shattered dreams: Brazil' on page 58, for each pair

Starter

1 Give the class in pairs the case study from Manchester, UK. Would they agree with Anthony or Jason, and why? Ask pupils to underline three or four key points. Ask for feedback and make a list of points on the board.

Activity

2 Hand out the Brazil case study to each pair to read. Pairs should then join with another pair. In groups they should highlight any similarities between the UK and Brazil case studies and then underline differences and decide whether overall the main message of each article is similar or not.

3 Ask for feedback from the class and discuss the similarities and differences. Does it appear that the same or different things are causing gun violence in Brazil and the UK? Which article had the greatest impact? Why? Which article was more effective in showing the human cost of arms abuse? Which article was more effective in looking at the causes of arms abuse? Who might the articles have been aimed at – young people, those who abuse guns, or the general public? Ask pupils to give reasons. Which article would be best at convincing young people to steer clear of getting involved in gun culture?

4 If 'gangsta rap' doesn't cause gun violence, what other things could be causing it? You could introduce other source material such as recent and relevant newspaper articles if you have time.

Closing discussion

5 If pupils could send a postcard to Camila in Brazil, what would they say and why?

Gangs and guns: who takes the rap?

Police in the North West [UK] are all taking part in the first national gun amnesty for seven years. *But we ask: will it stop the shootings?*

Gun crime in Greater Manchester [UK], (April 2001 to March 2002):

On the increase: guns seized in Manchester ▶

- 11 murders

- 84 serious woundings

- 639 incidents of violence involving guns

- 785 incidents of armed robbery

- 50 burglaries where guns were used.

For gang members in Manchester, guns have become the 'must-have' status symbol – even a fashion accessory. They're used in settling disputes between rival gangs, or turf wars between drug dealers.

But it's getting worse. Detectives say the gun-toting has led to 'disrespect' shootings in which people have been shot for as little as spilling a drink or laughing at someone's haircut.

The lyrics of gangsta rappers like So Solid Crew have also been blamed for popularising gun culture.

In Manchester, police, the council and other agencies have been taking a joint approach aimed at redirecting young people away from the gangs and into a better lifestyle...

But still the figures on gun crime continue to rise.

So what's the answer? Will a gun amnesty really stop the shootings? Is it fair to blame gangsta rap? What about better education and opportunities for young black men? How do you stop young people in gangs carrying guns?

Have your say

Anthony says:

66 Gangsta rap music is behind the rise in gun crime in inner city Manchester. As a DJ on a community radio station broadcasting to Moss Side, Hulme and Longsight, I ban bad language and gun music. I blame American pop artistes for driving communities – and sometimes families – apart. 99

Jason says:

66 Coming from a DJ, blaming music for the problems of gun crime to me is very disturbing. So he doesn't play music with bad language on his shows. So what? Other stations and even other shows on his station will. It is not the music that is behind gun culture, it is the people themselves. Can Anthony really sit there and say, 'yes, they heard So Solid, so they went out and got a gun and shot someone'? Be real. Pointing the finger at music and American pop artists is not the solution to this problem. You can even take off all gangsta rap and other music with bad language. Will that stop crime too? No. It is the people in these gangs, peer pressure, family values and social deprivation that are among the areas which need blaming. 99

(Source: www.bbc.co.uk/manchester)

Shattered dreams: Brazil

Every year, throughout the world, roughly half a million men, women, and children are killed by armed violence — that's one person every minute.

 ❝ I had plans for the future; I wanted to travel the world, take a modelling course, and continue my gymnastics training. My dreams were shattered. **❞**

Camila Magalhães Lima from Brazil

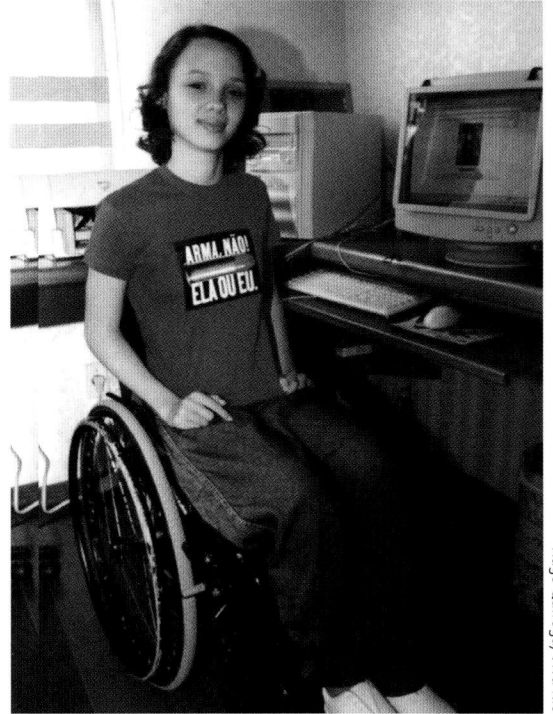

▲ Camila Magalhães Lima from Brazil

Sixteen-year-old Camila Magalhães Lima from Brazil lost the use of her legs in 1998, when she was hit by a stray bullet in a shoot-out between thieves and private security forces while walking home from school. In the 60 seconds it takes you to read Camila's story, it's likely that another two people, just like her, will have been seriously injured by the use of arms. Someone else won't have been so lucky. They're dead.

By 2020, the number of deaths and injuries from war and violence will overtake the number of deaths caused by killer diseases such as malaria and measles.

Without strict control of arms exports and measures to protect people from their misuse, countless others will continue to suffer the catastrophic consequences of the arms trade. Readily available weapons will intensify and prolong wars. More people will be terrorised and forced from their homes. Families will be prevented from growing food to feed themselves or earning enough money to send their kids to school. Human rights abuses will continue. People will be trapped in poverty. This isn't fiction. Oxfam and Amnesty International and IANSA members work with people who experience these atrocities every day.

The only way to end this cycle of poverty and suffering is to control the trade in arms. Now.

(Source: www.controlarms.org)

For more information about Camila, you can visit her website (**www.camila.lima.nom.br**).

Activity 4.4

Role-play: public inquiry

Objectives

- To explore a social and moral issue by working in role.
- To develop knowledge and understanding of some wider issues and challenges of global interdependence and responsibility.

Learning outcomes

Pupils will have:

- used a dramatic technique to explore the issues of the arms trade
- contributed to group work and exploratory class discussions.

You will need

- 'Public inquiry' on page 60, a set of roles cut up for each group

This activity is not aiming exactly to replicate the proceedings of public inquiries such as the Hutton Inquiry but acts as a device for discussing the topic of the arms trade. The aim is to give the proceedings a formal air and provide a structure for a variety of points of view.

You will also need to have carried out some work on the small arms trade prior to this activity, perhaps using the preceding activities in this section, or discussing source material from this and other chapters. You could also ask pupils to prepare in advance by asking them to carry out their own research on the small arms trade.

Starter

1 Introduce this activity by discussing the nature and purpose of public inquiries and any recent inquiries that have been in the news. Public inquiries are investigations held in public into aspects of a controversial proposal or situation.

Activity

2 Pupils should work in groups of six – each will run its own inquiry. The topic is 'Should the manufacture of and trade in small arms be banned?' Hand out the role cards to each group and explain the procedure. Five members of the group will take on a role each and the sixth member will take on the role of a judge presiding over the inquiry. The inquiry of each group could be named after the pupil presiding. You may wish to think in advance about who to appoint as judge, or let each group decide for themselves.

3 The role of the presiding judge is to introduce the proceedings, then hear a submission from each member of the group. The judge can question each participant up to three times. Each member of the group can ask questions of other members of the group but cannot question the judge.

4 The inquiry should last for a specified time – maybe 20 to 30 minutes.

5 Afterwards each judge should be given a short time to prepare a summing up of their findings and a recommendation on whether the manufacture and trade of small arms should be banned.

6 Each judge will then present their findings to the whole class.

Closing discussion

7 Carry out a debriefing. Did the judges all decide the same or not? Were pupils, once out of role, satisfied with the findings? Were any roles difficult to play and why?

8 Have a vote on whether the manufacture of and trade in small arms should be banned.

Public inquiry

Should the manufacture of and trade in small arms be banned?

A The Prime Minister
You want to make it absolutely clear that you have made a clear commitment to control the activities of arms brokers and traffickers wherever they are located. In fact it is in your party's election manifesto. You have made sure that improvements have been made to the way that arms are licensed for sale. To those that claim that UK arms have been exported to countries where they will be used to break international law, you want to point out that if the UK didn't sell weapons to a certain country, someone else would.

B Member of Parliament (MP)
You remember when this government came to power it made a big deal about saying that it would be honest and fair in its dealings with other countries. But you feel the government has been hypocritical on this issue. For instance, it has sold arms to Uganda and the Democratic Republic of Congo where four and a half million people have lost their lives in conflicts over the last five years. British companies are profiting from these deaths and you want to make it clear that there's blood on the government's hands over this.

C Citizen of Sierra Leone, Africa
Your point of view is that these arms manufacturers should be stopped. The world powers – the UK, France, the USA and so on, could help. After all, guns and rocket launchers aren't made for animals in the bush, so who are they being made for? To kill me and you! Arms are made to kill people. And to make it worse, you know that the diamonds from the diamond mines in your country, Sierra Leone, are being exchanged illegally for guns. You cannot understand why the arms sellers carry on when people's lives are being destroyed.

D Arms manufacturer
You're proud of your company and that it is helping to contribute to the security of the country. Every country needs to be able to defend itself and your company is producing cutting-edge technological components for today's modern defence systems. It's not as if yours is the only company – there are 1,135 companies in more than 98 countries manufacturing small arms, ammunition and components – and there are plenty of customers out there. You want to point out that you look after your many employees well and your very profitable business is contributing to the wealth of the country.

E Oxfam campaigner
You have been involved in researching the arms trade and you have discovered some shocking facts. For instance, from 1998 to 2001, the USA, the UK and France earned more income from arms sales to developing countries than they gave in aid. Oxfam thinks that the arms trade is out of control. Over 630 million small arms are in circulation and someone is killed through armed violence every minute. UK arms export controls are full of loopholes. For example British components were allowed to be exported to America, but were then used in planes sold to Israel that were used in raids on Palestine, killing civilians. It's time for an international Arms Trade Treaty with tough controls on the arms trade.

Further work and sources

These ideas allow further exploration of the causes of conflict and are suitable for projects, assignments or to be developed into a piece of English coursework.

1   This is an activity that could extend over a number of weeks and could be an assignment or developed into coursework. The main aim is to encourage pupils to consider the ways in which notions of conflict and weaponry can represent something 'cool' to be admired and desired. The activity will help pupils explore how images of combat are utilised in the world of advertising, fashion and designer living and their impact.

Pupils could carry out investigations into the way that combat and armed conflict images are used in different circumstances. Their investigations should lead to some sort of presentation or exhibition. This could be an exhibition board showing examples of the use of combat images with captions and annotations, or it could be a presentation or a song or video.

A questionnaire could be devised to establish how their peers, family, friends and members of the community view the 'accessorisation' of armed combat. It is important to avoid questions which only elicit yes/no answers and not to make the questionnaire too long. They should carry out a test run on three or four people and make sure that the questions make sense and that they are getting the type of answers they need. They should also think about how they are going to collate the information and set up a system, possibly a database system on computer, before they begin.

They should also start thinking about how they want to present their findings and put over their point of view. The 'exhibition' should make it clear where they stand. Pupils could present their 'exhibitions' to the class, including a piece on whether their views changed over the course of carrying out the work.

2   Pupils could design their own campaign or information poster on some aspect of small arms.

3   Pupils could summarise what they have learnt by writing a 100-word press release or a 300-word newspaper article on the impact of small arms on people involved in conflict.

4   There is source material in Chapter 7 showing how communities are working together to reduce violence and gun crime. Pupils could investigate initiatives in this country and other countries, such as the 'Million Mom' marches in the USA.

5   Pupils could write an essay outlining the arguments about whether rap influences young people and encourages violence, giving their own point of view with reasons.

6   Pupils could research the arms trade using websites such as the Control Arms campaign website **www.controlarms.org**, the Campaign Against Arms Trade website **www.caat.org.uk** (click on 'Information' and then 'Facts and figures'), and arms company sites such as the BAe site **www.baesystems.com**, the MBDA site **www.mbda.net**, the DRS Technologies site **www.drs.com** and the Heckler and Koch site **www.hkdefense.us**.

The effects of conflict

Reading for meaning, considering other people's experiences

Aims for this chapter

- To present some of the effects of armed conflict.
- To examine the ways in which armed conflict impacts on civilians.
- To analyse some personal responses to armed conflict.
- To explore some of the ways in which we learn about and make sense of the effects of armed conflict.

The case study

This chapter looks at Afghanistan as a case study of the effects of conflict and uses a boy's own story to convey information. The chapter also includes source material relating to Rwanda and Iraq and poetry relating to the Balkans. More information and personal testimonies on the effects of conflict in many other countries can be found on Oxfam's website at **www.oxfam.org.uk**. The skills, knowledge and understanding developed through the case study can be applied to other conflict situations and events.

Media reporting of the effects of conflict

The media coverage of conflict is a huge area of debate and comprises a number of different areas of discussion, including the way in which conflict is reported (for example by embedded journalists); propaganda; censorship; the extent to which the truth can and should be told in wartime; and the desirability and effects of watching coverage of violent conflict. There are many different possibilities for investigation and discussion and this chapter can only provide an introduction to the topic.

Activities in this chapter:

- Story-telling: it happened like this
- A journalist's view: community of enquiry
- Reporting the effects of conflict: fact and opinion

Activity 5.1

Story-telling: it happened like this

Objectives

- To use imagination to consider and empathise with other people's experiences.
- To respond to and critically evaluate creative responses to suffering.

Learning outcomes

Pupils will have:

- reflected on the nature and significance of the subject matter
- drawn inferences and made deductions.

You will need

- A copy of 'The effects of armed conflict on civilians' on page 64 for each pupil
- A copy of 'Afghanistan: country profile' on page 65 or an atlas or globe with Afghanistan clearly marked
- A copy of 'Juma's story' on page 66 for each pupil
- A copy of 'War poetry from various cultures' on page 67
- A copy of 'Corneille: from genocide survivor to international star' on page 68

Special sensitivity is needed if there are pupils in the class who have particular experience of conflict and war in some way, ether personally or in the family. Tell the class that they are going to be reading and listening to people's experiences of armed conflict and its effects. These will be conveyed in different forms – prose, poetry and visual image. They will be examining how conflicts affect people and how writers respond to and convey the practical and psychological effects, and they may find some of this disturbing.

Starter

1   Warn pupils that they will be dealing with difficult and disturbing issues. Give pupils in pairs copies of 'The effects of armed conflict on civilians' sheet on page 64 and ask them to read the information and then discuss which effects of conflict they think are shown in the picture.

2   Ask pupils for their reactions and discuss any points that pupils may find surprising or disturbing. The statistics are stark and horrifying but it is important to recognise that they are not just numbers on a page but things that have happened to real people, as the case study material exemplifies.

Activity

3   Explain that the focus of the activity will be on ways in which people are affected by armed conflict. The activity will use a case study from Afghanistan to look at the effects of war on civilians. Point out that the fact that civilians are more likely to be affected in armed conflict is one of the ways in which conflict has changed since the First World War.

4   Make sure all are clear where Afghanistan is located by using an atlas or the map on the Afghanistan country profile on page 65. You can also use the Afghanistan country profile to give some context and add to any knowledge pupils may already have.

5   Give each pupil a copy of 'Juma's story' on page 66, which they should read.

6   They can then devise a list of five or six interview questions and role-play in their pairs an interview with Juma about his life.

7   Ask a few pairs to perform their interviews for the rest of the class.

8   Discuss with the class how important it is for people to tell their stories about the effects of conflict. What different ways are there in which people can tell their stories, for instance by writing songs or poems, or painting pictures?

9   Read with the class one or more of the poems on page 67 or hand out the song by Corneille on page 68. Discuss with the class how the poems deal with particular effects of conflict, whether it is being a refugee (*Boy with Orange*), the dangers of living in a war-torn city (*Luck in Sarajevo*) or the psychological effects of being involved with conflict (*The hawk prays for peace* and *Alone in the world*). How does Corneille make something positive out of a difficult experience?

Closing discussion

10   Why might some people choose to write poetry or songs to tell their story about conflict and its effects?

The effects of armed conflict on civilians

How is modern conflict increasingly affecting civilians?

A. Warring parties are targeting civilians.

B. Men are conscripted or forced to fight by rebel groups.

C. Women and girls are used for sex, often at gunpoint.

D. Children are abducted and often forced to fight.

E. Refugees are robbed and abused, often at gunpoint.

Glossary

Conscription Making people join the armed forces to fight in a war. Governments usually conscript men between the ages of, say, 18 and 45 when they need more soldiers than they already have in the army.

- The uncontrolled increase of arms and their misuse by government forces and armed groups takes a massive human toll in lost lives.

- More than 500,000 people on average are killed with guns and other conventional arms every year – one person every minute.

- There are 300,000 child soldiers involved in conflicts around the world.

- Torture and ill-treatment by state officials – mostly armed police – went on in over 70 countries between 1997 and 2000.

(Source: www.oxfam.org.uk)

Did you know...

In the First World War 14 per cent of total casualties were civilian. In the Second World War this grew to 67 per cent. In some of today's conflicts the figure is even higher.

Geoff Sayer/Oxfam

◀ This picture shows the scene of a soldier and a captive, as painted by a child abducted in Northern Uganda. Children are particularly at risk of violence, coercion and deprivation in conflict.

Afghanistan: country profile

Population:
28.514 million

Area:
647,500 square kilometres
(UK 244,100 sq km)

Capital:
Kabul (1.4 million
inhabitants)

Life expectancy:
42 years

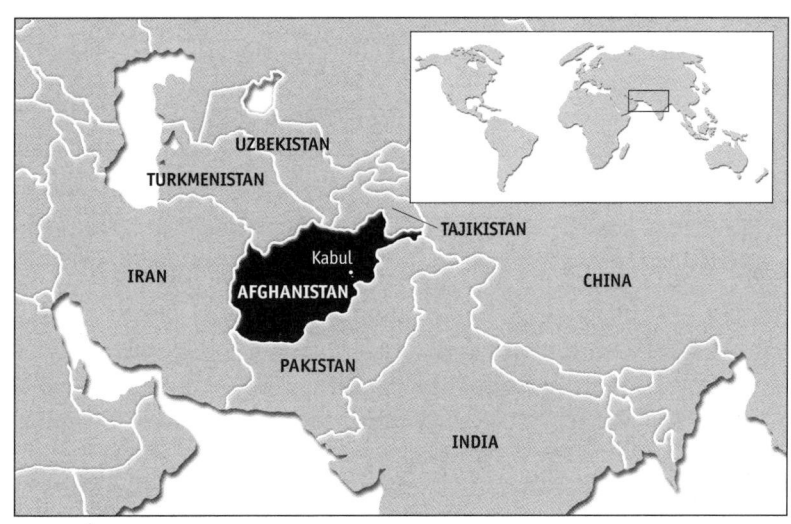

Afghanistan's recent history is a story of war and civil unrest. The Soviet Union invaded in 1979, but was forced to withdraw ten years later by anti-Communist forces supplied and trained by the USA, Saudi Arabia, Pakistan and others. The Communist regime in Kabul fought on until collapsing in 1992.

Fighting then erupted among the various factions. Rival military commanders used their own private militias to seize control of local or regional territory. Law and order broke down, creating conditions which eventually resulted in the growth of the Taliban. The Taliban developed as a political force and ultimately seized power in 1996. Following the 11 September 2001 terrorist attacks on New York, military action by the USA and some of its allies, including the Afghan Northern Alliance, toppled the Taliban.

In late 2001, a plan was agreed for the formulation of a new government. Hamid Karzai was elected President of the Government of Afghanistan under the new constitution in nationwide elections in 2004.

There is ongoing military action to root out remaining terrorists and Taliban elements and the country suffers from enormous poverty, a lack of skilled and educated workers, a crumbling infrastructure, and widespread landmines. However, many Afghan people are returning to contribute skills and rebuild their country.

> ❝ War is causing all our troubles. It has taken our schools and our houses and made us leave our land. The hospitals are ruined, the farms are destroyed, the children become orphans and the desperate families are forced to sell their children, the people become disabled and the women are left widowed and traumatised. The children are forced to work on the streets or go to Iran and Pakistan to find work. ❞
>
> **Street working child in Kabul, Afghanistan**
>
> (Source: www.savethechildren.org.uk)

Juma's story

Twelve-year-old Juma Khan lives in Zhare Dasht, a camp for internally displaced people. Situated 40km west of Kandahar, the camp is home to 30,000–40,000 people.

Juma came here after fleeing his home in Faryab province two years ago. 'People thought that we were Taliban, and we were threatened,' he recalls. 'So we left our villages and we travelled using animals and vehicles or by walking until we reached the border with Pakistan.'

When the bombing stopped, Juma Khan and the other refugees were taken to the camp at Zhare Dasht. He now lives in a small mud brick room with his grandmother. His father died fighting the Russians when he was a baby, and his mother died from a chest infection six years ago. An older brother works as a labourer in Pakistan. Another brother left to find work in Iran, but became a heroin addict and never returned.

Save the Children

Life at Zahre Dasht (which means 'yellow desert') is tough and uncertain. Despite extensive de-mining operations, mines and unexploded bombs litter the desert beyond the camp perimeter. 'I heard that two boys went to the mountains and saw part of a mine above the ground,' says Juma Khan. 'It exploded, and one of them injured his chest. The other one lost his hand. Another child stepped on a mine and was blown up.'

Juma Khan is also worried about the lack of educational opportunities for children at Zahre Dasht. Although there's a school at the camp, classes are held in large tents that are hot and dusty in summer and freezing cold in winter. There are few qualified teachers, and classes are overcrowded. It's especially difficult for girls, who are taught separately from boys. There are only two women teachers in the camp, and their classes number 120 pupils.

Children's schooling is also disrupted by the need to carry out hard work for the home. Most children spend several hours a day collecting water from communal pumps, or walking to the mountains to find firewood – an eight-hour return trip.

'There are three important things I'd like to see for children in Afghanistan,' says Juma Khan. 'First, children should leave unimportant work and go to school. Second, I want parents to allow children to attend school. And third, I want young people who are addicted to drugs to think of their homeland and to come back and help rebuild it.'

(Source: www.savethechildren.org.uk)

War poetry from various cultures

The hawk prays for peace

After my feathers have turned red
with the blood of victims,
after I have converted the moon into a nest
and filled it with the spoils of undeclared war,
after I have seized the arms of the armed
and disabled the fighting spirit of my youth,
after I have become the only bird
and all titles and praise names mine,
the sole proprietor of the world,
after I have become immortal,
let there be peace.

Tanure Ojaide (born 1948 in Nigeria)

Luck in Sarajevo

In Sarajevo
in the spring of 1992,
everything is possible:

you go stand in a bread line
and end up in an emergency room
with your leg amputated.

Afterwards, you still maintain
that you were very lucky.

Izet Sarajlić (born 1930 in Bosnia)
translated from the Serbo-Croat by Charles Simic

Boy with Orange (out of Kosovo)

A boy holding an orange in his hands
Has crossed the border in uncertainty.

He stands there, stares with marble eyes at scenes
Too desolate for him to comprehend.

Now, in this globe he's clutching something safe,
A round assurance and a promised joy

No-one shall take away. He cannot smile.
Behind him are the stones of babyhood.

Soon he will find a hand, perhaps, to hold,
Or a kind face, some comfort for a while.

Lotte Kramer (born in Mainz, she came to England as a child refugee in 1939)

Corneille: from genocide survivor to international star

Alone in the world

People often say that I look as if I have

Everything I want, but they don't know about

The ghosts which haunt me and

The requiems which I sing to myself.

I pretend to be tough every day which goes by

But the stones of every wall

Will break one day.

Perhaps I am the rock which people think I am

But I'm more fragile than you think.

Mother said to me before she left,

'Don't ever show your weaknesses

And if the worst comes to the worst,

Be strong and swallow your tears

Because your pride will be your best weapon'.

So I know how to laugh when I have to

But you mustn't think I fall apart when
no-one's looking.

I walk tall so that I don't bend

And I sing often

In order not to cry.

When I think of my life,

I face my nights.

Each day which dawns I say to myself that

I'm alone in the world

There's nothing I can do about it

I'm alone in the world

I can't stay silent about it any longer

I'm alone in the world

I feel lonely in the world.

**Extract from song written and perfomed by Corneille
Translation by Isabel Tucker**

Corneille's French R'n'B

Acclaimed as one of the hottest new arrivals on the French-speaking music scene, Corneille made a major impact with his debut album, *Parce qu'on vient de loin* (Because we've come from far away), released in February 2003. The Rwandan-born singer, now based in Montreal, has created his own individual style of French R'n'B, celebrating his new life after the tragic genocide in his homeland.

Given his first-hand experience of the Rwandan genocide, it is perhaps not surprising that Corneille has evolved into such a forceful personality. The singer freely admits that writing the songs on his album *Parce qu'on vient de loin* was a way of exorcising both collective dramas and his own personal nightmares triggered by a day in April 1994 when the army broke into his family home in Kigali. 'I lost my whole family that day,' says Corneille, 'My father, my mother, my brothers and my sisters were all wiped out while I was in the same room as them. I managed to escape the massacre at the last minute, diving down behind the sofa to hide. The soldiers never stopped to check whether their killing spree had spared anyone.'

After coming so close to death himself, the singer appears to have chosen to celebrate life in his music. But there's an undeniable political edge to his songs at times, too. 'My album's dedicated to all those who feel they've been ignored and overlooked,' Corneille declares. 'I've realised just how much injustice there is in this world. Take the events in Rwanda, for instance. OK, so the media reported the genocide in Rwanda – which was, let me remind you, the biggest genocide in the world since the Holocaust – but they made much more of a fuss about 11 September. You had all these different governments rushing to pledge help and support to the US, but those governments didn't lift a finger in 1994 during the Rwandan genocide. What's my new album? Definitely a celebration of my new life, but I never forget that countless people never had the right to that!'

(Source: Radio France Internationale)

Activity 5.2

A journalist's view: community of enquiry

Objectives

- To practise effective participation in group discussion and interaction.
- To gain insight into a journalist's perspective on reporting conflict.

Learning outcomes

Pupils will have:

- shown willingness to be open to changing their opinions and attitudes in the light of discussion and evidence
- examined how ideas, values and emotions are explored and portrayed.

You will need

- A copy of 'A boy called "Grenade"' on pages 70–71
- A map or globe with Rwanda clearly marked

Before you start you will need to arrange the classroom with a circle of chairs so that all pupils can see each other and the teacher. You may want to copy the story on page 70–71 so that every pupil has one to follow or you may prefer just to read it out yourself. You will need to have thought about the possible discussion questions that the story may generate and the sort of questions that you will ask to encourage the pupils.

Starter

1 Explain the format of the session to the pupils and that you will be reading them a story about a journalist and a boy who was a survivor of a terrible and tragic genocide that took place in the African country of Rwanda in 1994, when over 800,000 people lost their lives. Ask if anyone knows where Rwanda is and point it out on the map. You could use the Rwanda country profile on page 44 to give pupils some more information about Rwanda either now or during the course of the discussion.

2 Tell pupils that during and after the story you will want them to think of one or two questions which will help them understand the story better. You will then discuss one or two questions agreed on by the class.

Activity

3 Read the story to the class. The pupils think about and then note down questions based on anything they found interesting or puzzling about the story, factually or as a general issue.

4 They can share their questions with a partner first or you can ask for contributions from the whole class straight away.

5 Put the questions up on the board. Then sort them into factual questions and those that are more philosophical. You can put aside the factual questions to research later and concentrate on the more open-ended questions.

6 Ask the class to vote on which two questions should be discussed.

7 Agree on the conventions for discussion and what you want to get out of it. (See the Appendix on teaching controversial issues, page 102, for suggestions of how to set ground rules for group discussion.) You might wish to suggest that each contribution is prefaced with 'I agree with …' or 'I disagree with …'. Write up the ground rules on the board – e.g. everyone should listen and not interrupt; everyone is involved.

8 You will need to facilitate the discussion by asking searching or guiding questions. The discussion may be wide-ranging and you will need to decide whether to limit a particular direction and refocus.

9 If it has not already arisen, discuss the role of the journalist in wartime – what are the expectations that pupils have of journalists in wartime? Discuss how and why Fergal Keane has stepped outside this role.

Closing discussion

10 At the end of the discussion assess how well it has gone in relation to the agreed ground rules.

Philosophy for children

Philosophy for children is an educational movement which aims to promote children's thinking skills, curiosity, and overall intellectual and moral development by encouraging them to engage in philosophical enquiry in an unbiased and non-competitive way. The main forum for doing this is the 'community of enquiry', which develops as children read or listen to something, formulate their own questions and then discuss them. Ideally, the children should meet regularly to do this. This kind of philosophical enquiry helps children to respect each other, link their personal experience to more general issues and explore and challenge the views of others.

For more information, visit **www.sapere.net**

A boy called 'Grenade'

Kigali, Rwanda, April 1997

Today's correspondents meet many people who've suffered loss or been traumatised by war and violence. Sometimes it can prove an educational experience. This was the case when the author interviewed a young survivor of the Rwanda massacres which cost the lives of hundreds of thousands of people. He ended up questioning the very way he and other news-gatherers work.

Like nearly every other survivor of the genocide I have met, Placide always looked away when answering questions about what had happened to him. He did not look into my face, but rather into some unreachable distance, in whose limitless spaces he seemed lost. Yes, he could tell me his story and he could remember names, dates, places and incidents. But he would not meet my eyes and so that most fundamental of human contacts evaded me through the long hour I spent with him. Later, I would find out why. But only after I had made a very foolish and hurtful mistake.

We were sitting in the church, where he had seen his parents murdered, where he had seen children's heads smashed and pregnant women disembowelled, where he had seen what no child should ever see. And as I have done before in other zones of conflict, in other ruined countries, I listened, asked questions and recorded. He was patient with me. Most survivors are incredibly patient. But it was at the end of a day of stories, a day when the stories seemed to get worse and worse and by the end, sitting there in the church, I think I had started to lose my concentration. This is not by way of an advance apology for the mistake I made, but rather an explanation of how one can lose the sense of what one is doing.

You see, earlier in the day, somebody had told me that Placide's nickname was Grenade; this because he'd had a grenade thrown at him during the massacre and the shrapnel had badly marked his legs. I was given to understand that he liked the name, that he had laughed when someone mentioned it. It was background information, the kind of thing you store away and maybe or maybe not use when writing the script. But I decided to ask Placide about the nickname; it just might prove useful in building a picture of his life after the genocide.

'I understand you have a nickname,' I said. For the first time in the interview he looked directly at me. 'Is it true that your nickname is Grenade?' I asked. Placide's eyes began to fill with tears, in a few seconds he was crying uncontrollably. A soldier who had been helping us to interpret stood and took him by the hand and led him outside. I knew within an instant that my question had deeply hurt the child. Perhaps in front of his friends he had to pretend to like the nickname, but it was clear now that he felt ashamed, marked out and different because of his wounds. Grenade. The name singled him out and I, for the sake of one thoughtless question, had summoned up all of the pain it caused him.

A boy called 'Grenade'

I got up from my seat and walked out of the church, into a garden where, three years before, I had walked among the recently murdered bodies of Placide's family and hundreds of other local Tutsis. The bodies had been buried and a gardener had planted some brilliant yellow flowers along the pathway. Late golden African light played across the valley beyond. I could hear only birdsong and the quiet sobbing of the little boy. I began to think of the times I had faced other victims of violence and misery and asked them questions which had made them cry. It happens all the time in the world of news and current affairs. Reporters like me arrive in a place like Rwanda or Dunblane and we come into people's homes to hear and record their stories and many of them do weep and their testimony very often moves our audiences. But what happened with Placide has caused me to pause and question my questioning.

It has caused me to ask if the need to bear witness is worth the pain it can cause to others. For when we ask, 'How do you feel?' is it not a question calculated to probe and bring into the public domain the deepest emotions, and does the asking of such questions not impose upon us some responsibility for the emotional well-being of the person we are interviewing?

It is not the first time that I have asked this question, but never before has it been so acutely defined for me as in that Rwandan church. For I move on as other reporters elsewhere move on. But the people whose grief we disinter are left to their lives and memories. In my case, the reporting of genocide and man's inhumanity to man has brought me professional praise and awards and many letters of thanks from my listeners and viewers. But you must forgive me if I say that in the Rwandan church I felt ashamed of myself and the hurt which my question had caused. Of course, the world in which I work is full of difficult questions, questions which often demand an answer. But let me say only that Placide has reminded me to think carefully before opening my mouth; he has reminded me that humanity must come before everything else.

by Fergal Keane
from *Letters Home*, Penguin Books, 1999, © Fergal Keane

Activity 5.3

Reporting the effects of conflict: fact and opinion

Objectives

- To evaluate the media's role in society in providing information and affecting opinion.

Learning outcomes

Pupils will have

- looked at how meaning is conveyed
- distinguished between fact and opinion, bias and objectivity.

You will need

- Copies of 'Shoot now, think later' on page 73 for each pair

Starter

1 Ask pupils to read the article in pairs and insert the phrases at the bottom in the appropriate spaces. (This activity helps reading for meaning.)

2 Discuss the results of this and give the correct answers.

Activity

3 Pupils could pick out six key words that help convey the message of the article and choose the key sentence.

4 Pairs of pupils should then read the article again and highlight or underline the facts and the opinions in it in different colours.

5 Suggest that pupils discuss the following questions. Is there more fact or more opinion? Is this surprising? Does the article set out to be a factual article or is its purpose to present a point of view? How do you know? Was it difficult to work out the point that the journalist is making? What does he think of the coverage of the war in Iraq? How could his style of writing be described? Is it serious or flippant or ironic? How can you tell?

6 Ask for feedback. Discuss how the article presents a point of view – there is more opinion than fact and the words chosen suggest strong feelings about the subject, e.g. 'lousy reportage'. Discuss whether the writing is biased.

7 Discuss any images that pupils do not understand. What images does the writer use that relate to conflict and battle? What images does he use that relate to everyday life?

8 There are references to powerful images from the Iraq war such as the pulling down of Saddam Hussein's statue but are these images still current? Are there visual images that pupils may be aware of relating to conflicts in history, such as the return of Chamberlain from Munich, the burning child in Vietnam, the Chinese student trying to stop the tank in Tiananmen Square? Discuss what is meant by an iconic image and what part such images play in our understanding of past conflicts.

9 How much impact does journalism have on public understanding of and attitudes to conflict and war? Pupils should be encouraged to refer to recent reporting.

Closing discussion

10 Brainstorm the responsibilities of journalists. Do these responsibilities remain the same in war and peacetime? What is meant by the famous quotation 'The first casualty of war is truth'?

11 Have a show of hands on whether journalists should always tell the complete truth in wartime.

Answers to the word gaps

1 hitting their targets 2 a virtual game 3 the horrific action 4 the causes and motives
5 endless numbing footage 6 in our living rooms 7 gasping excited commentaries
8 continuous forward momentum

Shoot now, think later

The chic philosopher Jean Baudrillard famously stated that the 1991 Gulf War never happened. ... Baudrillard was talking about the anaesthetising effects of broadcast news; real conflict in 1991 was turned into animated computer game, encouraged by Pentagon briefings that focused on graphically generated images of bombs _____.

Because we were denied the close-up reality of war, we felt detached. It was like watching a battle on Playstation and the language of 'collateral damage' and 'softening up' convinced us we were participating in _____ .

Conversely, the second war [in Iraq] brought us too much reality. Rolling news coverage and embedded reporting took us, apparently, right into the heart of _____ .

And yet the coverage of this war was noted for both its inaccuracy and lack of objectivity. If we were getting facts around the clock, why did so many of those facts prove inaccurate? Given we were being taken into the heat of battle, why was our understanding of _____ of the war confused, and why were political opinions never fully analysed?

Perhaps because our interpretation of the war was once again conditioned by the favoured media format of the moment. Programmed over the past few years to watch _____ of ordinary people trapped by television producers in an artificial situation, we, the viewers, felt we were watching Reality TV on a massive scale. As Rageh Omar, John Simpson and Bill Neely [TV journalists] swapped smart suits for combat gear, we realised we were watching a People Show. Rageh and John and Bill were Jo Public, ordinary bods whom we'd had _____ _____ once or twice a week over the past few years. Now we were watching them placed in a hostile environment, and have cameras pointed at them 24 hours a day while a whole nation gawped and took bets on which one would crack the most. ...

The decision to embed reporters with troops led to great footage but lousy reportage. No reporter, his or her life literally being protected by the military round them, was going to file a report saying 'the troops I'm living with are disgruntled. Their equipment doesn't work, they're probably blowing up children, and one or two of them are going to die.' Instead, objectivity melted faster than a division of the Republican Guard, and these seekers of the truth were reduced to _____ _____ such as 'over there, some bastard Iraqis are firing on us'... .'

Everything is a selection. Even live coverage is subject to the whim of a news editor who chooses the most exciting location from which the coverage should come. But the popularity of rolling news has forced emphasis on the immediate at the expense of the longer overview. ...

The urge to provide a _____ _____ to news coverage meant that dull casualties had to be left behind where they had fallen. The need to fill our schedules with breaking action, with fresh troops of information, plus the automatic reflex action of the broadcasters that, once the war had started, it was our war, that it was against an 'enemy', and that it was about 'liberation', led to a total breakdown of intelligent and dispassionate analysis. Hence, a battle that had started on the basis that there were horrific weapons of mass destruction to be found, was, by common consent, ended when a statue was toppled and, with it, all hope of objectivity.

Armando Iannucci, *The Guardian*, 28 April 2003

Phrases for the gaps

A. the horrific action
B. hitting their targets
C. the causes and motives
D. continuous forward momentum
E. endless numbing footage
F. gasping excited commentaries
G. a virtual game
H. in our living rooms

Further work and sources

These ideas allow further exploration of the effects of conflict and are suitable for projects, assignments or to be developed into a piece of English coursework.

1   Many men, women and children have tried to express the pain of conflict and the horror of war in a creative way. Some of these representations of war through the arts have helped those who have not been involved in war and armed conflict to understand what it might feel like. Pupils could research examples of conflict and war in an aspect of the arts, such as painting or play-writing. They could choose examples that work for them particularly well and explain why.

2   Groups could look at the poems and extracts and pictures in this chapter and discuss their impact. Think about how the impact is made – which words are particularly powerful? Are the words and images emotive or factual? Does the impact lie in the strength of the imagery? Relate this to work that pupils may have carried out on the poetry of the First World War or the history of the Second World War.

3   One effect of conflict is that people, communities and countries can be divided. People are made to seem 'other'. This is seen at its most extreme in cases of genocide such as the Holocaust, or the genocide in Rwanda, and in the ethnic cleansing in the Balkans. This is a difficult subject, but some pupils may be interested in thinking about how it happens and considering how it can be guarded against in our society today.

4   You could ask the pupils to carry out some investigative coursework looking at change and continuity in conflict and its effects on civilians. The investigation would centre on how older people in their community perceive conflict and the changes in conflict that have taken place during the last century. Discuss with pupils how such an investigation might best be carried out. Would it be through interviews, questionnaires or informal discussions? How many people would they like or be able to talk to? Who could they ask? How might they be approached? Are there other sources of information that they could use, such as websites or the school library? How would the results best be written up and presented?

5   Pupils could investigate child soldiers by visiting and researching websites of agencies such as Oxfam, Save the Children, UNICEF and CAFOD.

6   Fergal Keane and other journalists who reported the genocide at the time have visited Rwanda since and written personal and extended pieces of journalism. Pupils may like to read some of these reports which can be tracked down through the BBC news website **http://news.bbc.co.uk** and through the websites of national newspapers and news magazines.

Resolving conflict

Reflecting on rights, debating the rules

Aims for this chapter:

- To raise some issues of conflict resolution and international peacekeeping.
- To provide some starting points for exploring conflict resolution at different levels – individual, community, national and international.

The case study

This chapter is about rights and responsibilities that we all have and the way in which they can be used as part of peace-building. Timor Leste (East Timor) – the world's newest nation (in 2002) – is used as a case study to look at the use of peacekeeping forces as part of conflict resolution. The activities in this chapter can be adapted to explore other conflict situations in the world and the solutions that may be available.

Activities in this chapter:

- The right way to peace?
- Keeping the peace?
- Healing the wounds

Activity 6.1

The right way to peace

Objectives

- To raise issues of human rights and responsibilities.
- To recognise the importance of resolving conflict fairly.

Learning outcomes

Pupils will have:

- used information processing skills
- examined and discussed ideas, values and emotions.

You will need

- A copy of 'Talking about it' on page 77 for each pair
- A copy of 'Human Rights, Children's rights' on page 78, for each pair
- A copy of 'The United Nations' on page 79, for each pair

Glossary

Negotiation Negotiation is the process by which agreements are reached in a non-violent manner. The countries involved in the discussion will try to reach an agreement by talking through the key points of the conflict. It usually involves a mediator and compromise.

Starter

- Ask pupils to look at the pictures in the source material 'Talking about it' and to talk in pairs about what is happening in the pictures.
- Ask them to relate these pictures to things that happen in their own school. What are the positive benefits of talking and working together with others?

Activity

- Ask pupils in pairs to draw up a list of the ten most important rights that all human beings should have.
- Then say that they can only have three of these rights – which would they be?
- Ask them to read the brief list of human rights and children's rights on page 78. How similar are their own lists of rights? They should follow this by talking about how these rights could be upheld.
- Give pairs of pupils the information on the United Nations to read. How can the United Nations ensure that countries adhere to its rules? Pupils could discuss parallels at different levels: e.g. rules at school, laws in the community. Does the United Nations work in the same way? What part do responsibilities play?
- Ask for feedback from the class. Then discuss what happens in international conflict situations. Does the United Nations have a role to play here? Can they think of any examples of the United Nations working in conflict areas or helping to keep the peace?
- You could introduce for discussion a relevant newspaper article or show a video of a news clip about a UN peacekeeping mission. Pupils could list three benefits and three disadvantages of such a mission.

Closing discussion

- How does the work of the United Nations relate back to their first discussion about the pictures and talking together? Introduce the word 'negotiation' and discuss its meaning.

Photo information

The photos show pupils at school in Botswana and Thailand.

Talking about it

Panos/Giacomo Pirozzi

Panos/Jeremy Horner

Making Sense of World Conflicts

Human rights

The **United Nations Universal Declaration of Human Rights** (1948) states that 'all human beings are born free and equal in dignity and rights' and are entitled to 'life, liberty and security'. Some of the other rights are:

- The right to vote to choose your government or political representatives without having to tell anyone how you vote
- The right to freedom of assembly, to meet with people and form or join groups as you wish
- The right to freedom of belief and expression
- The right to have equal treatment regardless of race, sex, language, religion, political opinions, nationality or social class
- The right to life, liberty and security
- The right to freedom of movement within your country, and to leave and return to your country
- The right to live in dignity, with a standard of living that ensures health and well-being for you and your family.

Children's rights

The **United Nations Convention on the Rights of the Child** (1959) gives children rights, including:

- The right to affection, love and understanding
- The right to adequate nutrition and medical care
- The right to free education
- The right to full opportunity for play and recreation
- The right to a name and nationality
- The right to special care, if disabled
- The right to be among the first to receive relief in times of disaster
- The right to be a useful member of society and to develop individual abilities
- The right to be brought up in a spirit of peace and universal brotherhood
- The right to enjoy these rights, regardless of race, colour, sex, religion, or national or social origin.

The United Nations

The United Nations was established on 24 October 1945 by 51 countries committed to preserving peace through international co-operation and collective security. Today, nearly every nation in the world belongs to the UN and membership totals 191 countries.

When states become members of the United Nations, they agree to accept the obligations of the UN Charter, an international treaty that sets out basic principles of international relations. According to the Charter, the UN has four purposes:

- to maintain international peace and security
- to develop friendly relations among nations
- to co-operate in solving international problems and in promoting respect for human rights
- to be a centre for harmonising the actions of nations.

The United Nations is not a world government and it does not make laws. It does, however, provide the means to help resolve international conflicts and formulate policies on matters affecting all of us. At the UN, all the member states – large and small, rich and poor, with differing political views and social systems – have a voice and a vote in this process. It is the only major forum where countries of the 'South' can outvote countries of the 'North'.

The countries are obliged to keep to certain regulations:

- All member states are equal.
- Conflicts between countries should be resolved in a peaceful manner.
- The member states are not allowed to use violence or threaten to use violence.
- The UN should not interfere with domestic problems.

The United Nations has six main organs – the General Assembly, the Security Council, the Economic and Social Council, the Trusteeship Council, the Secretariat and the International Court of Justice.

All UN member states are represented in the **General Assembly** – a 'parliament of nations' which meets to consider the world's most pressing problems. Each member state has one vote. In recent years, a special effort has been made to reach decisions through consensus, rather than by taking a formal vote.

The **Security Council** has the primary responsibility for maintaining international peace and security. The Council may convene at any time, whenever peace is threatened. Under the Charter, all member states are obligated to carry out the Council's decisions.

- Fifteen countries are members of this council.
- Five countries are permanent members and these are:
  China, France, Russia, the United Kingdom, the United States
- Ten other countries are members for two years at a time
- All countries have an opportunity for membership

Decisions of the Council require nine 'yes' votes. Except in votes on procedural questions, a decision cannot be taken if there is a 'no' vote, or veto, by a permanent member.

When the Council considers a threat to international peace, it first explores ways to settle the dispute peacefully. It may suggest principles for a settlement or undertake mediation. In the event of fighting, the Council tries to secure a ceasefire. It may send a peacekeeping mission to help the parties maintain the truce and to keep opposing forces apart.

The Council can take measures to enforce its decisions. It can impose economic sanctions or order an arms embargo. On rare occasions, the Council has authorised Member States to use 'all necessary means', including collective military action, to see that its decisions are carried out.

(Source: www.un.org)

Activity 6.2

Objectives
- To generate ideas and suggest hypotheses.
- To examine peacekeeping solutions.

Learning outcomes
Pupils will have:
- examined and discussed ideas, values and emotions.

You will need
- A copy of 'Timor Leste (East Timor): country profile' on page 81 for each pupil
- A copy of 'Keeping the peace in Timor Leste' on pages 82–83, for each pupil
- A map or globe

Keeping the peace?

You may wish to ask pupils to read the material beforehand in preparation for this activity.

Starter
1   Ask the class if anyone knows where Timor Leste (East Timor) is and point it out on the map or globe.
2   Pupils should then read the country profile. Clarify any points necessary.
3   Do a spot quiz on Timor Leste.

Activity
4   In pairs, pupils should read and discuss 'Keeping the peace in Timor Leste'.
5   Discuss with the class the reasons why there was hesitation on the part of the United Nations to intervene. Do pupils think this was justified? What criteria might the United Nations use when deciding whether to send peacekeeping forces? (See 'The United Nations' on page 79 for more information about this.)
6   Pupils should then use the case study material to plan a five-minute TV report on the situation in Timor Leste as it was after the election in 1999, including coverage of the peacekeeping force. They should write a 30-second introduction. They should then note down who they will interview, the questions they will ask and the kind of film coverage or pictures they would like.
7   Alternatively pupils can write newspaper reports – a third of the class writing for an Indonesian paper, a third for an East Timorese paper, and the rest for a UK paper.

Closing discussion
8   Display the newspaper reports or act out the TV reports, if there is time. Briefly discuss any issues arising.

Timor Leste (East Timor): country profile

Population: 924,642

Area: 14,874 square kilometres
(UK: 244,100 sq km)

Capital: Dili

Religion: 90% are Roman Catholic,
while the rest are Muslims or follow
traditional religions. Many Catholics
practise traditional religions
alongside their Catholicism.

Life expectancy: 57 years

Climate: Tropical with heavy
rainfall.

Environment: The island is
mountainous with an extensive river
system. It used to be covered with
dense rainforest, but there has been a lot of deforestation which has
caused soil erosion and flooding. The southern region is flat and suitable
for agriculture. The main crops are coffee (which is exported), maize (the
main staple food) and rice. Timor Leste is heavily dependent on adequate
rainfall both for agriculture and for drinking water, which makes it
vulnerable to drought and climate change. There are gas and oil reserves
offshore which are expected to provide economic growth in the future.

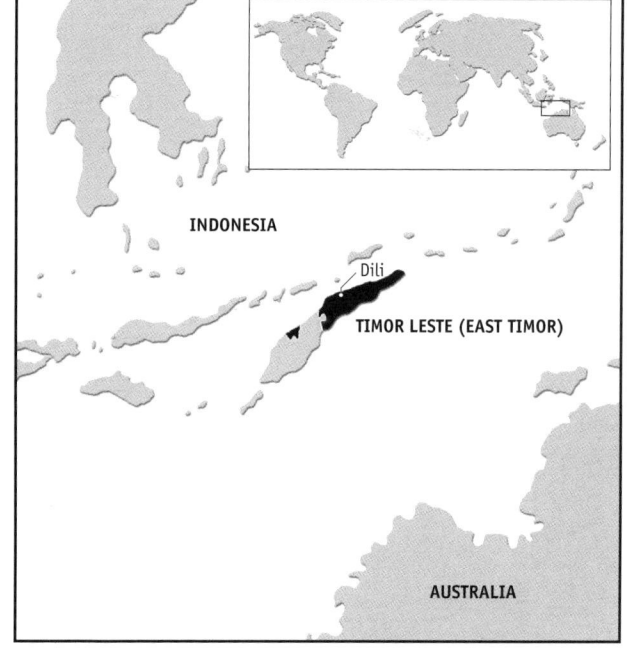

Timor Leste occupies the eastern part of the island of Timor, with an
enclave in the western part of the island called Oe-cussi. Most of the
western part of Timor island is part of Indonesia.

Timor Leste (the official name meaning East Timor) or Timor Lorosae 'Land
of the Rising Sun' is one of the world's newest nations, officially gaining
independence on 20 May 2002 when it became the 191st member country of the
United Nations. Formerly a Portuguese colony, Timor Leste was invaded by
Indonesia in 1975. In the next 25 years of Indonesian occupation it is
estimated that 200,000 Timorese died. Since then, life has improved
slightly in Timor Leste. The East Timorese people are working to
reconstruct their country by improving living standards, agriculture and
education.

Keeping the peace in Timor Leste – 1999   Part 1

Timor Leste votes to become independent

On 28 November 1975, Timor Leste became independent from Portugal. Shortly afterwards it was invaded and occupied by Indonesia. The countries of the United Nations (UN) demanded that Indonesia withdraw and passed a number of resolutions but Indonesia did not take any notice. Apart from a few exceptions, the international community did not apply any further pressure to Indonesia.

Over the next 24 years, the Indonesian army caused much conflict, suffering and death in Timor Leste, but according to their own rules, the UN could not send a force to deal with the situation without permission from Indonesia.

Finally, President Habibi of Indonesia announced that the East Timorese people would be allowed to vote in a referendum on becoming independent. On 30 August 1999 the people of Timor Leste voted overwhelmingly to sever ties with Indonesia after 24 years of armed occupation.

Violence erupts

Soon after President Habibi's announcement, pro-Indonesian armed groups were threatening, assaulting and even killing people who were in favour of independence. The acts of violence continued and increased after the referendum. Many people were killed or forced to flee and Dili, the capital city, was destroyed. Many other buildings on the island were also destroyed.

Thousands of people had to flee into Indonesian West Timor; others escaped into nearby mountains where they had to eat plants and roots to survive. Many people lost their homes and all their belongings.

'There is no sign of normal life,' said one eyewitness in Dili. 'The streets are almost deserted but for some stray pigs and dogs. There is no food anywhere in the city. The pavements are strewn with loot, piles of boxes, refrigerators, TV sets, sofas, thousands of plastic chairs and even a grand piano.'

What happened next?

Was a UN peacekeeping force the answer?

The derelict market in Dili. It was destroyed during the conflict in 1999. ▶

Annie Bungeroth/Oxfam

Keeping the peace in Timor Leste – 1999   Part 2

International debate

There was international debate about whether the UN should send in a peacekeeping force.

Some said YES...

❝ The international community must act now or regret yet another tragedy it could have prevented. ❞

Mary Robinson, the UN High Commissioner for Human Rights

At the outset of this crisis, some called for an international force to be sent to Timor Leste as, the Indonesian army itself was involved in the violence instead of defending people. After a week of unrest, the 15,000-strong Indonesian army had managed to arrest only 27 militiamen.

It was argued that the killings in Timor Leste justified international action as Timor Leste was not recognised as being part of Indonesia and the East Timorese people had voted for independence.

Some said NO...

❝ The deployment of peacekeepers may well exacerbate the situation and be counterproductive, however well-intentioned. ❞

Makarim Wibisno, Indonesian ambassador to the UN

Some countries believed that Timor Leste and Indonesia should be left to sort out their own problems and feared that the arrival of a peacekeeping force could actually increase violence from the militias as they realised they were no longer in control of the area.

It was also argued that because Indonesia was in the process of transition to a more democratic system, forcing the government to accept international intervention might create a backlash, with Indonesians becoming more nationalistic and the army becoming even stronger.

What happened next?

Finally, under pressure from foreign countries, Indonesia agreed to the UN sending in a peacekeeping force two weeks after the elections. The Security Council agreed that the force could `take all necessary measures'. The peacekeeping force was led by Australia.

What the media were saying

Some Western media were criticised for failing fully to report the problems in Timor Leste for years: 'For almost 20 years, the BBC and other major Western news agencies preferred to 'cover' Timor Leste from Jakarta (capital of Indonesia), which was like reporting on a Nazi-occupied country from Berlin' (John Pilger, *The Guardian*, 7 September 1999). The media in the USA and the UK were criticised for failing to report fully their countries' involvement in Indonesia's past, including the sale of arms, and for not recognising Timor Leste as a country.

One of the probable reasons this region did not get media attention at the time of the referendum was because of the amount of investment there from richer countries – Indonesia owes billions of dollars to Japanese, American and European Banks. These countries wanted to ensure that they got their investment back.

(Source: Adapted from Global Express © DEP – Manchester Development Education Project Ltd.)

Activity 6.3

Healing the wounds

Objectives

- To consider the importance of resolving conflict and maintaining peace.
- To explore social and moral issues through texts.

Learning outcomes

Pupils will have:

- examined and discussed ideas, values and emotions
- contributed to group discussions and interaction.

You will need

- A copy of 'What is peace?' on page 85 for each group

Starter

1 Read this poem out and ask the class what the message is:

No peace in the world without peace in the nation;
No peace in the nation without peace in the town;
No peace in the town without peace in the home;
No peace in the home without peace in the heart.

(From the *Tao te Ching*, an ancient Chinese text)

Activity

2 Ask pupils in pairs to try to come up with their own definition of peace.

3 Each pair should then join with another pair to discuss their definitions and make one combined definition.

4 Hand out to the groups the quotes about peace and the poem on page 85, and ask them to choose the three quotations that link most closely with their definition of peace.

5 Suggest they read the poem out loud and then discuss what it is about and what it means. They should then choose a quotation that links with the poem or echoes what it is saying. What do they think of the other quotations?

6 Ask for feedback from the groups and discuss the definitions and choices made.

7 The poem was written in response to the 11 September 2001 attacks in the USA. It was written by Ben Okri, the Nigerian writer who won the Booker Prize for *The Famished Road*. What do the class think the message of the poem is?

8 When a country and people try to rebuild their lives after conflict, there is a need to build – or rebuild – trust and respect between former enemies. One word for this process is reconciliation. How important is reconciliation to maintaining peace? What are the benefits? What does it involve? Why is it difficult? What gets in the way? What are the steps to achieving it? What are the costs of not achieving it? Does justice always require that someone be punished?

9 Pupils could write their own poems on the theme of peace and reconciliation, which could be finished for homework if necessary.

Closing discussion

10 Pupils could choose their favourite quotation and be ready to explain the reasons for their choice.

What is peace?

'Peace is not merely a distant goal that we seek, but a means by which we arrive at that goal.'
Martin Luther King Jr., USA

'I wondered why somebody didn't do something, for peace, then I realised, I am somebody.'
Anonymous

'Establishing lasting peace is the work of education; all politics can do is keep us out of war.'
Maria Montessori, Italy

'Every gun that is made, every warship launched, every rocket fired, signifies in the final sense a theft from those who are cold and are not clothed.'
Dwight Eisenhower, USA

'Without Justice, peace is nothing but a nice sounding word.'
Dom Helder Camara, Brazil

'There is no way to peace, peace is the way.'
Mahatma Gandhi, India

'If you want peace, prepare for peace.'
University of Peace, Costa Rica

'If you want to make peace with your enemy, you have to work with your enemy. Then he becomes your partner.'
Nelson Mandela, South Africa

'Peace should be the future for the children of Africa.'
Mwjuma (14), Congo

'Peace comes from within. Do not seek it without.'
The Buddha

'You will never understand violence or non-violence until you understand the violence to the spirit that happens from watching your children die of malnutrition.'
Food First

'After the bombing I saw people getting caught up in their bitterness and the past. People were divided and were happy to stay that way. No child should ever be exposed to living amongst such attitudes of hate and bitterness.'
Margaret Gibney, Northern Ireland

'Never doubt that a small group of thoughtful committed citizens can change the world. Indeed – it's the only thing that ever has.'
Margaret Mead, USA

'Peace grows from inside people and from the community they live in.'
Sopheap (18), Cambodia

'Peace comes from the heart.'
Peter (11), Burundi

(Source: How do we make peace? (Discussing global issues series) Unicef UK)

Grief

Grief ought to be used
To create more love;
There's no greater force
From below or above.

Such grief as we have seen
Could water the roots
Of a new world dream.
Give the dead the power

To change the world
Into something higher;
That we may listen to hunger's
Cry and turn injustice into a flower.

This is the strange blessing
Of those flaming towers:
That we may wake up to world suffering
And with vision sweeten humanity's hours.

Ben Okri

Further work and sources

These ideas allow further exploration of conflict resolution and sources and are suitable for projects, assignments or to be developed into a piece of English coursework.

1   The following letter appeared in *The Guardian* on 7 April 2004.

'In April 1994, the world's media was accused of largely ignoring the Rwandan genocide. The same cannot be said of the tenth anniversary. Over the past few weeks a steady flow of journalists has been passing through Kigali and on to memorial sites around the country. While it is vital that the events of 1994 are never forgotten, many of us working and living in Rwanda have been saddened that there hasn't been more coverage of the positive stories. For example, that 720,000 more students are registered for primary school than in 1994 and secondary school attendance has increased five-fold. I hope that after today's anniversary we will read as much about Rwanda's future as its past'.

Phil Hudson, Country Director, VSO, Rwanda.

Pupils could do research using websites, such as Oxfam's and those of other aid and development agencies to look for stories of hope and recovery. They could write a 'positive' news story for a newspaper focusing on present successes and future plans. This could be linked to work carried out for other chapters in this book such as on resolution and peace-building.

2   Pupils could carry out a simulation of a United Nations General Assembly to discuss the possibility of sending in a peacekeeping force into a part of the world where there is conflict. This can be quite a large undertaking but there is plenty of support and material available from the United Nations Association for creating a 'Model Assembly'. Schools around the country have carried out such simulations, often making a day event, working with other schools and booking the Town Hall or other suitable venue. Go to the United Nations Association website **www.una-uk.org** and click on 'Model UN Events and Ideas'.

3   Find and read poems about peace. Pupils could write their own peace poems.

4   Groups of pupils could research 'conflict resolution', 'peer mediation' and 'buddying', and then make recommendations for how conflicts in schools could best be resolved. They could present their recommendations at the school council.

5   Pupils could research the work of the Truth and Reconciliation Committee in South Africa and then present their findings to the rest of the class.

Bringing about change

Planning to persuade, participating in action

Aims for this chapter:

- To consider ways in which communities and countries can move ahead in the aftermath of conflict.
- To provide opportunities to explore, design, plan and evaluate action for change.

The case studies

This chapter looks at bringing about change. The case study material picks up on the case studies used in previous chapters and shows how each of the countries or regions is taking action for change and involving local people. There is also material from the Control Arms campaign which shows how Oxfam, Amnesty International and IANSA (The International Action Network on Small Arms) are working together to bring about a change in the international laws on the small arms trade. This can also be used as a case study of how voluntary organisations (NGOs) set up and run campaigns, and the way in which they appeal and persuade. The skills, knowledge and understanding developed through these case studies can be applied to action, campaigning and reporting the aftermath of other conflict situations and events.

Activities in this chapter:

- Role play: citizen or truant?
- Futures
- Planning a campaign
- Peace journalism

Activity 7.1

Role-play: citizen or truant?

Objectives

- To explore issues of rights and responsibilities.

Learning outcomes

Pupils will have:

- used a dramatic technique to explore an issue
- worked co-operatively to synthesise information and test hypotheses.

You will need

- Copies of the scenario and role cards from 'Citizen or truant' on page 89 for each group.

This is a an activity sequence which is likely to take more than one lesson and has therefore been split into two parts for ease of planning. You need to think in advance about how you will construct the 'action tree' in part two of the activity.

Starter

1 To begin with pupils should get into four groups and discuss the scenario of the role-play on page 89 and one particular role per group. So one group will discuss the Bo role and each member should have a Bo role card, while another group will discuss Jay and each group member will have a Jay role card. Ask them to think and talk about how the role would be played. This will help those who are less confident in role-play.

Activity – part one

2 Split the pupils into new groups. Each group should be made up of four pupils – one from each of the four different original groups, so that each group of four pupils comprises the four different roles.

3 Tell pupils that the four characters happen to meet in the school at a parents' evening shortly before the planned march. Groups should then role-play the situation for about 15 minutes.

4 Ask a few groups to perform in front of the class.

5 Pupils should then come out of role and discuss in their groups how they felt about the character that they played.

6 Discuss with the class whether the arguments put forward by the groups were similar. Was the outcome of each role-play similar or different?

7 Ask pupils to vote on which outcome was the most positive.

Activity – part two

8 Recap the role-play scenario and discuss the outcomes of the role-plays. Ask the whole class to suggest ways that people could get involved in the campaign without going on a march.

9 Create an 'action tree'. Lay out the shape of a tree in the middle of the floor, or on a large table using large sheets of paper, or draw one on the board. Write the issue – campaign for arms control and an end to gun violence – in the trunk. Write or make symbols for the possible actions and display these as fruit; for ways of achieving the actions as branches; and for the resources needed to do this (e.g. skills, materials, contacts) in the roots.

10 Use the tree as a basis for discussing the local and global effects of each action, the power needed to make the changes and how the class might be able to help. Ideas can be added around the tree.

Closing discussion

11 If the role plays ended with winners and losers, how could the outcome be a 'win/ win' situation so that all involved felt that the outcome was reasonably fair? Discuss with pupils whether they think there is a 'correct' solution.

Citizen or truant?

Scenario

There is a poster up in a shop window in the local area advertising a march and rally to draw people's attention to the huge numbers of people dying in armed conflicts and from gun violence. This is said to be partly due to the spiralling arms trade and numbers of small arms in communities around the world. The march will call for greater control of arms and is taking place next Wednesday morning in the centre of town – a school day.

You are Bo, the twin of Jay

You are aware that there are at least 30 armed conflicts going on all over the world; many of them are forgotten but people are dying every day. You have learnt that trading arms is big business and that there are around 639 million small arms and light weapons in the world today. Eight million more are produced every year. You read in the local paper that someone was shot by a gang member in an area not far from you and you are very concerned. It all links up and you know that you must do something! In your citizenship and other classes you have discussed the importance of democracy and the right of freedom of expression – including taking action. You know that a lot of your friends feel strongly too.

You are Jay, the twin of Bo

Of course you are concerned that innocent people are getting shot but people are also dying in earthquakes and floods, and there are innocent animals getting hunted and killed. There are loads of things in the world that are terrible but you can't go and march about them all otherwise you would never be in school. It's all very well learning about how to be a good global citizen but at the moment you've got enough hassle at home to be getting on with. Anyway, if the kids who want to march feel that strongly about gun violence, why do they spend so much time playing 'Deathdoom' on their computers?

You are a parent of Bo and Jay

You opposed the war in Iraq and you are appalled when you read of the terrible atrocities carried out in conflicts around the world. You are worried by the local gun crime. You absolutely agree with a ban on people carrying handguns. You think it is important for young people to understand politics and get involved in the community. In fact, you would go on the march yourself if you could. At the same time, you don't want to encourage your child to get into trouble at school by walking out and you don't feel you can write an absence note.

You are a teacher

Although you have some sympathy for the cause and are concerned about the increase in violent crime locally you do not feel that children can be allowed out of school to go on a demonstration. You have heard that at least 20 pupils are planning to walk out of lessons and join the march. If the school doesn't make a stand and punish any pupils who are absent without leave – truanting – then it will set a precedent, and pupils could be walking out of school for all sorts of reasons. There are important exams soon and the year group needs to be focused.

Activity 7.2

Futures

Objectives

- To think constructively and empathetically about our global future.

Learning outcomes

Pupils will have:

- examined, hypothesised about and discussed non-fiction material
- developed skills of enquiry and communication.

You will need

- A copy of one of the case studies on pages 91–94 – Manchester, Cambodia, Brazil or Sierra Leone – for each pupil or pair of pupils.

Starter

1   Give pupils as individuals or in pairs one of the case studies. They should read the case study and highlight up to three actions that have been taken to bring about change for the better.

2   Take feedback and check that everyone understands their case study.

Activity

3   Pupils should then imagine that it is ten years in the future and that they are journalists visiting the country of their case study to find out what happened and how successful the people were in continuing to bring about change.

4   They can discuss in pairs what they think they find. If time allows, they should then write a newspaper article dated ten years into the future reporting on the situation in the country and the success of the projects. They should include brief interviews and a picture.

5   Pupils then get into groups of three or four with pupils who have been looking at the same case study. They should pool ideas or read and discuss their newspaper reports.

6   Ask each group to list three or four things which (either in real life or in their newspaper articles) helped ensure that things changed for the better in their case study. Examples could include the fact that Patsy and Sheila took advice from people with experience of their problem (Manchester), or the fact that the concert was shown on television (Cambodia). Groups should feed their lists back to the class.

Closing discussion

7   If they wanted to campaign to change something, what methods and strategies could they use? How would they go about this?

Children's radio in Sierra Leone

Marian Magdalene Bangura, a 17-year-old radio presenter from Freetown, Sierra Leone, says:

❝ Radio is important for children, especially for children who do not have a voice. It is very important for the girl child. It's important for children to make programmes so they can show their talent, not just go to school. Also, they can share their knowledge and skills and it's very interesting to hear their voice on the radio. Parents encourage children to learn things on the radio, you can listen to what is going on in the country. ❞

Radio is an excellent way of educating and engaging people, especially in countries where literacy levels are low and newspaper distribution generally confined to urban areas, but where almost every family has access to a radio.

▲ Children interviewing other children in Sierra Leone

▲ Recording a radio programe

After years of civil war, a radio project in Sierra Leone is trying to help children and their families return to a normal life. Plan UK (**www.plan-uk.org**) is working in partnership with local communities to establish Moyamba District Children's Awareness Radio (MODCAR), a child-led community-based radio station. Moyamba is a rural region of Sierra Leone with a population of 420,000.

Many children and young people in Sierra Leone missed out on their education during the recent war, and through this radio station they will be able to alert adults and their peers to the importance of gaining a good education to ensure a return to normality. They will also be able to share important information on such topics as HIV/AIDS and reproductive health, about which there is currently no popular resource for children and young people.

Children will use the radio station to express their feelings on the war and how it affected them. The station will also help to raise awareness amongst children and adults of children's rights and responsibilities.

❝ Radio is important to us, we want to communicate with other children. There are programmes we want to tell other children about; if there is a problem in maths, a child can go on the radio and explain the difficulties. We can explain rights and responsibilities that are relevant to children. As we have just come out of the war, children attend school and many are still traumatised; radio helps them understand things better. Adults will have their own programmes too: they will have agriculture programmes that will help farmers to know when to apply fertilisers, ❞

says Mohamed, 17, a student representative for the MODCAR radio project.

(Souce: www.plan-uk.org)

Making Sense of World Conflicts

Taking action against arms abuse: United Kingdom

Mothers' war on gangland shootings

Two mothers whose sons were victims of gangland shootings in Manchester are campaigning for an end to gun crime.

Together they helped set up Mothers Against Violence (MAV) to support victims' families.

Patsy McKie and Sheila Eccleston travelled to Boston, United States, last year, to find out how American methods are curbing street crime. In the USA police patrols intervene and mentor young gang members before they get sucked into a life of crime.

With 200 people injured and 25 dead in Manchester in the last four years, Patsy and Sheila set up a similar scheme closer to home. The scheme in Greater Manchester uses two specially appointed street workers rather than the police to go out into communities.

Mrs McKie's son, Dorrie, who had never been in trouble with the police, was shot dead in 1999, but nobody has been charged with his murder. Sheila's son, Dean, was shot and killed almost two years ago in Longsight, Manchester. Police say his death was gang-related but no one has been charged with his murder.

Patsy and Sheila hope the MAV group will get to the heart of the problem and spare other mothers the heartache they have gone through.

(Source: http://news.bbc.co.uk)

Mothers against guns

I am a poet, daughter, sister, mother. This is something I wanted to share. Peace needs to begin in our hearts to reach the streets...

A mother to her children

This fragile world we live in, the trials that we face
the children scared of living, they pull guns they don't embrace.
As mothers of these children,
we fear to let them go.
You think you have prepared them,
but then you never know.
The torment that you live with,
the fear that clouds your days.
These children what can we give them,
to make a brighter day?
It's always in a mother,
to love with her whole heart.
In hope her child may follow...

be strong, be wise, be smart!!

Ms L Lovell

(Source: Black Information Link, www.blink.org.uk)

Cambodia: campaigning for change

Pajaree/Oxfam

◀ Women at Phnom Penh Central Market drawing their own faces to add to the Control Arms petition. More than 73,000 faces have been collected in Cambodia.

The Cambodian government has given its backing to Control Arms – the international campaign of Oxfam, Amnesty International and IANSA (the International Action Network on Small Arms) to push for an international treaty on the trade in weapons.

In Cambodia this campaign is desperately necessary. As a result of its 30 years of war the country is awash with weapons, perhaps as many as one million – one for every eight adults. And though Cambodia's government is working hard to rid the country of this plague, every day at least two or more Cambodians are killed or injured in incidents involving firearms.

On the launch day in October 2003 about 450 people gathered in the Cambodian capital Phnom Penh for the three-kilometre march, bearing banners, posterboards and balloons, through the city's busiest streets. The march ended with a concert at a large outdoor stage in the riverside Hun Sen Park. Massive banners on either side of the stage proclaimed 'The Arms Trade is Out of Control', and 'Control Arms'. The park grew thick with people, peaking at about 10,000.

Broadcast live by Cambodia's national television station and interspersed with popular Cambodian music and dance performances, the concert's messages included more strong statements of support by senior government representatives.

Will the world pay attention to Cambodia's voice of experience as this small country, flooded with arms by the superpowers during its 30 years of war, takes a stand against the arms trade?

(Source: www.oxfamgb.org/eastasia/cambodia)

Viva Rio, Brazil

In December 2003 Viva Rio celebrated the 10-year anniversary of its activities. Viva Rio was set up in Brazil to combat rising violence and gun crime and to work for peace. It carries out projects in Brazil and internationally such as the COAV (Children in Organised Armed Violence) project in 12 countries where there is significant involvement by children in armed violence – Jamaica, El Salvador, Ecuador, Honduras, the Philippines, Sierra Leone, Nigeria, South Africa, Haiti, the USA, Northern Ireland and Colombia. These projects are examples taken from their website **www.vivario.org.br/english**.

Villa-Lobinhos

Villa-Lobinhos provides quality musical instruction to talented young musicians between the ages of 12 and 20 from *favelas* (shanty towns) and low-income communities. The students involved receive transport vouchers and a contribution to personal expenses. They take part in various classes and activities, including individual and ensemble work as well as information technology classes. They are invited to perform for the public at charity events held in Rio de Janeiro state concert halls, and instructional mini-concerts at the Villa-Lobos Museum.

Children's Hope Space

The Children's Hope Space is a permanent Viva Rio project operating in a *favela* complex of Rio de Janeiro. It is seeking to foster a culture of peace and active citizenship among young people, and to help them to fulfil their potential by providing access to sports and artistic and cultural activities along with access to the internet.

At present the project involves 2,000 young people enrolled in a wide variety of courses, including swimming, football, basketball, volleyball, theatre and dance. In addition, the Children's Hope Space Library, fitted with 32 computers with internet access, serves an average of 6,000 people per month.

'Enough! I want peace!' campaign, July 2000

Promenade to call people for the 'Enough' demonstration in Copacabana.

Activity 7.3

Planning a campaign

Objectives:

- To explore social and moral issues through print and ICT-based texts.
- To analyse ideas, to suggest hypotheses, to apply imagination.

Learning outcomes

Pupils will have:

- judged the value of their own and others' work and ideas
- used creative thinking skills.

You will need

- A copy of the Control Arms campaign material on pages 96-97 for each pair
- A copy of the 'Action card game' cards on page 98, cut up for each pair

Starter

1 Give out copies of the Control Arms campaign material to pairs of pupils and explain that it is taken directly from the website of the Control Arms campaign, which is run jointly by Oxfam, Amnesty International and IANSA (International Action Network on Small Arms).

2 Give pupils ten minutes to assess the overall impact of the campaign material. Ask pupils to ring up to five words, phrases or images that they think create this impact.

Activity

3 The following discussion with the class will explore the meaning of 'campaign' and how the campaign material uses persuasive writing and factual argument to make a case for arms control.

4 What is the main aim of the Control Arms campaign? Is it clear? Discuss the key phrases or sentences that explain the aim. Are the words or the pictures more important?

5 Who does the class think is the audience for this piece? Are they persuaded? Would they be moved to find out more or to take action having read this? Why?

6 What were the main campaign actions taken on the launch day to draw the issue to public attention? Why might these actions have been chosen?

7 Pupils should now consider persuasive campaigning in a wider sense and imagine that they have decided to become involved with the campaign. There are now two ways to continue the lesson depending on pupils' familiarity with the issues.

    Either:

8 Pupils should prepare a three-minute speech on the Control Arms campaign to try to persuade others in the school and community to get involved. They can use the website material and if they have carried out other activities from this book they can add other information about arms and gun control. They can make their speeches.

    Or:

9 The mission is to persuade others of the importance of this issue and to choose a campaign action to carry out, having discussed the advantages and disadvantages of a variety of different actions.

10 Give pairs of pupils copies of the Action cards cut up from the 'Action card game' sheet on page 98.

11 Pairs of pupils should arrange the nine cards in a diamond pattern. They should put their preferred action at the top and the least preferred at the bottom. In between will be a row of two, a row of three, which have little to differentiate them, and then another row of two.

12 Groups should then feed back their top and bottom choices and these should be noted on the board.

Closing discussion

13 Either:

    Discuss which speeches were the most effective.

    Or:

    Discuss the results. As a class, try to come to a consensus on which action would have the most impact and which action could be most easily undertaken by the class, bearing in mind the following: think big but start small; set realistic goals; be prepared to work hard; use the specific talents of the people in the group; get more people involved.

Taking a stand:
what the Control Arms campaign says

Oxfam, Amnesty International, and IANSA (The International Action Network on Small Arms) have launched a campaign to lobby for greater control on arms. This is part of the campaign information found on the website **www.controlarms.org**.

The issues

Uncontrolled arms fuel poverty and suffering

There are around 639 million small arms and light weapons in the world today. Eight million more are produced every year.

Without strict control, such weapons will continue to fuel violent conflict, state repression, crime

Giovanni Diffidenti/Oxfam

and domestic abuse. Unless governments act to stop the spread of arms, more lives will be lost, more human rights violations will take place, and more people will be denied the chance to escape poverty.

For many years, in our work around the world, Oxfam, Amnesty International and IANSA have witnessed the human cost of arms abuses and campaigned for tougher arms controls. But now the situation is critical.

Urgent measures are needed immediately. Governments need to take action at every level, from communities to the international arena, to stop this suffering.

Spiralling out of control

" Children come out of school talking about guns. The mentality is so much more vicious now. They don't talk about beating each other up. They talk about killing each other. "

Former youth worker in north London, 2002

From the inner cities of the UK to the pastoralist communities of Kenya, gun culture is on the increase. In countries where carrying weapons is traditional, bows and arrows have been replaced with new, deadlier weapons. There are more arms than ever before — and now they're cheaper than ever too.

Taking a stand:
What the Control Arms campaign says

The problem

Crispin Hughes/Oxfam

❝ A gun is as easy to get as a packet of cigarettes. ❞

Evan Jean Lolless, 34, serving life imprisonment for murder in the USA, 1997

The issue is simple. The unregulated supply of weapons makes it easy for criminals to murder, for soldiers to kill indiscriminately, and for police to take lives arbitrarily. Today's weapons are quicker and more powerful than ever before. And in the wrong hands, faster and more powerful weapons mean more abuse and more wasted lives.

It's not just unlawful killings during wartime that are on the increase. Military and security equipment is being misused by soldiers, paramilitaries and police to kill, wound, and commit terrible atrocities against civilians during peacetime too.

The global misuse of arms has reached crisis point.

The flow of arms to those who openly flout international human rights and humanitarian laws is being ignored by many governments and companies. Guns especially have never been so easy obtain. Their increased availability threatens life and liberty in communities and cities around the world. Including yours.

The solution

The time to act is now; face up to the arms crisis!

We won't achieve anything without you. We need you to join the Control Arms campaign here. Today. It's your world. Take action now.

Campaign launch

Control Arms launch day – 9 October 2003 – was unique. On this day hundreds of thousands of people across continents and countries of the world announced that arms are out of control. Newspaper headlines, radio stories, street marches, symbolic gravestones, personal testimonies, interviews with government ministers and celebrities ... were all designed to have maximum impact and not go unnoticed.

Action card game

The best action is to put our arguments to (lobby) someone in a powerful position, eg write a letter or an email, send a petition or an opinion survey, visit them.

It could be your head teacher, MP, someone from the council in charge of facilities for young people.

The best action is to find out which organisations can help us, and join their local, national or global campaigns.

The best action is to perform a play on how the issue affects people, eg *in assembly, feeder primary schools.*

The best action is to invite a guest speaker into school to talk about the issue, or to be part of a debate.

The best action is to make a leaflet, poster or collage on the issue and display it to people in school and in the local community.

The best action is to make different choices about your life based on what you have learnt, eg change what you eat, wear and spend money on. Other people will notice and follow your example.

The best action is to make a video, audio or photograph presentation to provide discussion about the issue, and get people to debate it.

The best action is to raise money and donate it to a charity working on the issue.

The best action is to work with the press, eg talk on local radio, invite them to an event.

(Source: *Get Global: A Skills-based approach to achieve global citizenship.* Key stages 3 & 4, © ActionAid)

Activity 7.4

Peace journalism

Objectives

- To evaluate the way language is used.
- To reflect on the power of the media.

Learning outcomes

Pupils will have:

- exploited choice of language and structure to achieve a particular effect.

You will need

- A copy of 'War and peace journalism' on page 100 for each pair

You will need to ask pupils to bring in headlines from the newspapers about an armed conflict, or provide some yourself from the internet or the press. You will also need copies of a short report on a contemporary conflict.

Starter

1   Pupils should work in pairs using the contemporary newspaper headlines. They should decide whether their headline promotes the possibility of peace or focuses on the aggression and conflict between the sides. They should underline the key words.

Activity

2   Get feedback – check what pairs think and how many headlines fall into each category. The probability is that there will be more focus on conflict. Discuss with pupils why they think this is the case. Discuss the values of the media: controversial stories attract attention; conflict, whether between individuals or states, is high on the list and if the story involves a VIP, celebrity or someone glamorous, so much the better.

3   Give pupils copies of the 'War and peace journalism' sheet and discuss the two example headlines, the quotation and the proverb. What do they mean? Do pupils agree with these points of view? You could work with the whole class taking one or two of the headlines discussed earlier to rewrite from the opposite point of view – to promote peace (or highlight conflict).

4   Have a look at the six suggestions for what a 'peace journalist' would do, and discuss them.

5   Give pupils a short newspaper report on a contemporary conflict and ask them to rewrite it as a 'peace journalist' might. Or ask them to write their own report from scratch, on a local or other conflict, as a 'peace journalist' would.

6   Read some of these reports out.

Closing discussion

7   Discuss whether they think 'peace journalism' would be a useful contribution to reducing conflict in the world? Do they think that peace journalism would catch on?

War and peace journalism

A World leaders plead for sanity in Middle East meltdown

Prospects for Middle East peace lay in tatters last night after the worst day of violence in the occupied territories since trouble erupted a fortnight ago.

B 'Peace – now more than ever,' say Arabs and Jews as death toll inches up

Middle East peace campaigners redoubled their calls for dialogue last night after violence in the occupied territories caused widespread destruction to property and claimed two more lives.

▲ Examples of press coverage are based on actual coverage since 2000

❝ Journalists have a big responsibility in crises like these. ❞
Danny Schecter, www.mediachannel.org

❝ Until lions have their historians, tales of hunting will glorify the hunter. ❞
African proverb

❝ Media coverage including photography can have a very positive effect on the lives of individuals in countries such as Iraq and Afghanistan. But sadly, and all too quickly, after a crisis the media often vanishes. ❞
Nick Danziger, freelace photojournalist

What a Peace Journalist would try to do

1 AVOID concentrating always on what divides the parties, the differences between what they say and what they want. INSTEAD try revealing areas of common ground and leading your report with answers which suggest that some goals may be shared.

2 AVOID only reporting the violent acts. INSTEAD show how people have been blocked and frustrated or deprived in everyday life, as a way of explaining the violence.

3 AVOID blaming someone for starting it. INSTEAD try looking at how shared problems and issues are leading to consequences that all the parties say they never intended.

4 AVOID focusing only on the suffering, fears and grievances of only one party. INSTEAD treat as equally newsworthy the suffering, fears and grievances of all sides.

5 AVOID 'victimising' language such as 'pathetic' and 'tragedy'. INSTEAD report on what has been done and what could be done by the people. Don't just ask them how they feel, also ask them how they are coping and what they think. Can they suggest any solutions?

6 AVOID vague use of emotive words to describe what has happened to people, and avoid adjectives such as 'brutal' and 'barbaric'. INSTEAD always be precise about what you know. Do not minimise suffering but reserve the strongest language for the gravest situations.

(Source: *Peace journalism – how to do it* by Jake Lynch and Anabel McGoldrick)

Further work and sources

These ideas allow further exploration of bringing about change and are suitable for projects, assignments or to be developed into a piece of English coursework.

1   Invite a journalist into school and get the class to prepare an interview which covers issues of the values of the media, whether journalists have responsibilities and can make a difference, 'forgotten' conflicts, and 'peace journalism' and whether it is the way forward. Write up the interview into an article for the school magazine or website, and edit it to reflect the journalist's particular point of view.

2   Using the radio project in Sierra Leone on page 91 as a starting point, pupils could try writing an episode of a radio soap set in a country that has experienced conflict. If pupils are not familiar with *The Archers* or similar, record an episode and listen to it first, discussing the style of writing, the tone, the characters and so on; note how much happens with the plot in one episode. Alternatively, use *EastEnders* or another TV soap that pupils are familiar with as a model for an episode of the soap. This could become a longer project incorporating research into the use of radio in developing countries.

3   Using the Control Arms campaign material reproduced on pages 96–97 and on the campaign website **www.controlarms.org**, pupils could look at how the campaign material sets out to persuade people of its point of view and the methods it uses to encourage people to join in the action. Look at language – which are the key words? What part do the pictures play? How are the website pages presented in terms of the amount of information, and the use of testimonial and case studies? What about the balance of facts and opinion? Pupils could write an extended critique saying how effective they think the campaign is and why.

4   The aftermath of conflict throws up many dilemmas and difficulties for governments and citizens. There are different ways of dealing with what has happened, one of the most famous being the Truth and Reconciliation Committee in South Africa. Pupils could research this approach to conflict aftermath and compare it with what is happening after other conflicts such as those in Afghanistan, Iraq and Timor Leste.

5   Pupils could research literature and poetry from a country that has experienced conflict. This can be done by using search engines or visiting sites such as **www.sierra-leone.org/culture.html** Analyse and compare the poetry. Read some of the literature. Does the poetry deal with reconciliation issues and action for change? Pupils could write an essay on the findings.

6   Pupils could research what young people are doing to work for peace by visiting the Peace Child website at **www.peacechild.org**, and some of the links. Pupils could work in pairs to identify the key challenges that young people face when working for peace locally, nationally and globally, and then prioritise what they themselves can do. They could then consider ways that they can build bridges, and overcome cultural differences and prejudices about these. Then they could do a presentation or plan and carry out some campaigning.

Appendix: Teaching controversial issues

Controversial issues unfold across our TV screens 24 hours a day. Every day, teachers snatch conversations about the headlines, playgrounds buzz with rumours and concerns, parents discuss their hopes and fears, and pupils ask their teachers difficult questions and may even walk out of school to demonstrate on the streets. Controversial issues fuel much of our daily conversation and affect our daily lives.

Seemingly distant events can affect us closely and controversial issues are evident in many aspects of our lives, even the apparently mundane. If you ask any group of teachers to pick an item in the news or even a topic from the syllabus and rate it zero to five on a 'controversy spectrum' you may be surprised how few get a zero. Try it!

Controversial issues and English

Language enables us to communicate ideas and discuss issues and to explore the complexities of our lives. In English pupils study fiction and non-fiction texts which cover a vast range of human experiences – many of them will be challenging. Pupils will study classic and contemporary texts and explore social and moral issues. They will learn to make articulate and perceptive comments on them. In so doing, they will inevitably need and want to deal with the controversial issues. The following section will help teachers prepare for this.

What makes an issue controversial?

'Issues that are likely to be sensitive or controversial are those that have a political, social or personal impact and arouse strong feelings and/or deal with questions of value and belief.'[1] Examples are sex education, religion, politics, family lifestyle and values, law and order, financial issues, unemployment, environmental issues, bullying and bereavement. Controversy arises when different groups offer conflicting explanations, based on differing values, about what has happened and why, what should happen and how to achieve it. Such issues cannot be settled by facts or evidence alone. Global issues will often be contentious and involve a range of views, interests and values. Wars and armed conflicts are by their very nature controversial, with the opposing sides feeling that their lives and way of life are at stake.

Why is it important to teach about controversial issues?

Life and the way we live it are controversial! Pupils should not be sheltered from difficult issues – it is important for them to clarify their emotions and values and to learn to think for themselves. As the Commission on British Muslims and Islamophobia suggests, 'It can in fact be reassuring to children and young people, as distinct from merely alarming or depressing, to be reminded that their elders are in disagreement with each other about important matters. It may be more important for them to live with differences and uncertainties rather than settle for oversimplified solutions.'[2] The knowledge, skills and attitudes developed through engaging with controversial issues are central to helping young people become effective citizens of the 21st century world.

- Controversial issues are a stimulus for learning. Discussing hot topics engages young people, is relevant and creates a sense of responsibility.
- A range of teaching and learning styles and methodologies can be used, including role-play, creative writing, drama, visual arts, debate, enquiry, presentations and simulations.
- There is the potential to challenge stereotypes, widen horizons and explore alternative viewpoints in a safe environment.

- Young people can develop participative skills of discussion, learn the rules and conventions of argument and debate, weigh up evidence, learn to distinguish between fact and opinion, choose from alternatives, and deal with conflict.
- Discussing controversial issues can help promote thinking skills.

How are controversial issues best handled?

Many teachers will actually have actually dealt with a range of contentious issues as a matter of course, as they have arisen in the classroom or corridor. But there is still some concern when it comes to teaching a 'Controversial Issue'. This usually connotes a topic that can engender very strong emotions and feelings. Effective handling of this in the classroom starts with some basic strategies:

- Ensure that pupils establish ground rules about how they will behave towards each other, such as no interrupting and no racist, sexist or mocking comments. Agree on what happens if the ground rules are transgressed.
- Ensure that pupils have access to balanced information and differing viewpoints, including input from visitors where possible, to help clarify their own opinions and views.
- Suggest that pupils discuss issues in small groups, if greater confidentiality is deemed necessary, and give support to these groups when it seems desirable.
- Encourage everyone to express their views and opinions (but do not put pressure on them) and make sure all are properly heard and respected.
- Recognise that the teacher is in a powerful position and decide whether, how and when to express personal views.

The principle of the freedom of thought and expression, a value enshrined in the Declaration of Human Rights, can be referred to. However, pupils may well ask how this works alongside the agreed ground rules and the right not to be threatened or abused. In practice, the law often puts the right of a person to live in peace and security higher than the right of another person to express themselves in insulting or threatening ways. This is appropriate to most circumstances including schools and classrooms. For example, racism and bullying are never acceptable.

There will be different classroom contexts needing appropriate strategies – monocultural and multicultural, all-white, classrooms with refugee children, classrooms with a range of religions represented and those within faith schools. There is no substitute for knowing your classroom context from experience but there are some pointers to bear in mind:

- Vocabulary is important, should be used knowingly and may be valuably discussed. 'Different' does not mean 'worse than'. 'Different' is a term to be used positively. Diversity is valuable and positive. We learn from difference and diversity. 'Other' as a term can be explored. Everyone is 'other' to someone just as everywhere in the world is 'local' to someone.
- Sensitivity is needed, of course. Pressure should not be put on children to contribute publicly experiences related to controversial issues. Small group work may be more appropriate than whole-class discussion when dealing with controversial issues.
- It may be difficult for pupils to contribute their particular point of view in a situation where peer pressure is in play. In this case, working with the points of view of others in an activity such as a role play is a useful strategy.
- Ground rules are very important and if drawn up by the class at the beginning create ownership of the activities or discussion. The class can then regulate its own learning process.

What about bias?

One of teachers' greatest concerns is how to avoid bias and maintain balance. The Education Act 1996 aims to ensure that children are not presented with only one side of political or controversial issues by their teachers. This is not intended to be paralysing but as a reminder of the influential position of the teacher and the need to be mindful of teaching approaches. Teachers should not shy away from topics because they will not be able to cover every minute aspect. By adopting the strategies below they can create an open forum where a range of ideas, views and opinions can be explored.

Teachers can:

- teach pupils how to recognise bias, evaluate evidence, seek different sources of information, and give reasons for their views and behaviour
- avoid presenting information as though it is not open to qualification or questioning and interpretation
- avoid presenting opinions and value judgements as facts
- think carefully about balancing the selection of material to be used
- use first-hand information where possible and resist giving their own interpretation of others' accounts and views
- put material in its historical, geographical and cultural context where possible
- tell pupils where the material has come from – for example, who has written it, and for what purpose or audience.

Teachers must choose their own role as appropriate. For example:

- The teacher acts as a chairperson allowing all viewpoints to be represented through pupil contributions or other inputs and materials, but does not state their own position.
- The teacher expresses their own views at the start, so that pupils can evaluate bias, but then goes on to make sure all views are presented.
- The teacher makes sure all views are presented, but concludes by stating their own position, underlining the need for pupils to evaluate all viewpoints before forming their own opinions.
- The teacher plays 'devil's advocate' to make sure that all views are covered if a consensus of views needs challenging.

Teaching controversial issues lends itself to active and participative teaching methodologies. Using literature, art and music can be a powerful way to help young people explore their own and other people's viewpoints, feelings and experiences. This book encourages the use of such methodologies.

Controversial issues and thinking skills

Teaching controversial issues goes hand in hand with developing thinking skills which can be strengthened though the approaches described above and by using the suggested activities. Reading challenging material and discussing social, moral, political, and cultural issues encourage pupils to develop the skills below.

Information-processing skills

These enable pupils to locate and collect relevant information, to sort, classify, sequence, compare, contrast, and to analyse part/whole relationships.

Reasoning skills

These enable pupils to give reasons for opinions and actions, to draw inferences and make deductions, to use precise language to explain what they think, and to make judgements and decisions informed by reasons or evidence.

Enquiry skills

These enable pupils to ask relevant questions, to pose and define problems, to plan what to do and how to research, to predict outcomes and anticipate responses, to test conclusions, and to refine ideas.

Creative thinking skills

These enable pupils to generate and extend ideas, to suggest hypotheses, to apply imagination, and to look for alternative innovative outcomes.

Evaluation skills

These enable pupils to evaluate information: to judge the value of what they read, hear and do, to develop criteria for judging the value of their own and others' work or ideas, and to have confidence in their judgements.

1 *Citizenship: A scheme of work for Key Stage 3* Teacher's guide, Qualifications and Curriculum Authority, 2001

2 *Talking and Teaching*, Commission on British Muslims and Islamophobia, undated.
   www.runnymedetrust.org/meb/islamophobia/talking_teaching.html

Glossary

Arms brokers Arms brokers are the middlemen often involved in arranging arms deals between countries. A broker will source the arms from the most suitable country or countries and arrange all the necessary paperwork on behalf of their client. Brokers are usually based in different countries from their clients. For example, a broker based in a European country could be arranging a deal for a customer in Africa, and sourcing his weapons in Eastern and Central Europe. Brokering can also involve a range of related activities including transport and financial services associated with the deal.

Arms transfer A term describing the movement of arms. International arms transfers involve the movement of arms from one country to another.

Asylum seeker A person who has fled their country and is seeking refugee status in another country.

Civilian A person who is not a member of the armed forces.

Civil war A war between citizens of the same state.

Cold war A struggle for precedence between Communist and non-Communist powers after the Second World War.

Compromise Each side in a conflict will probably make demands. A compromise is when either or both sides agree to change their demands so that both sides can accept a solution. If neither side is prepared to compromise there will not be a diplomatic solution.

Conflict In this book, 'conflict' is used to mean armed conflict at any level. This includes international war and also civil war, insurgency, guerrilla war, low-level fighting in the aftermath of conflict and violence in communities.

Diplomatic solution If one or both sides in a conflict would rather not use violence or indeed if neither side thinks it could win or the cost of winning would be too high, then the two sides usually start talking to see if they can agree on how to resolve the conflict without violence.

Disarmament Reduction by a state of the number of its national arms and weapons.

Elections A time when people (the voters) can vote for a person (or candidate) to represent them. Usually there are many candidates for the voters to choose from. This can happen at national level but also for local government and within societies, schools etc

Ethnic cleansing Action taken by a state or by an armed group to drive out or kill other people of a particular ethnic or religious group.

Ethnic group A group of people who share a distinctive culture and sometimes a common racial origin. Where such a group forms a minority of the population (there are fewer of them than of another ethnic group) they are known as a minority ethnic group.

Export licensing Arms deals invariably need special government approval before the sale can go ahead; this is known as an 'arms export licence'. Arms manufacturers will apply for an export licence from the appropriate government department and the sale will only proceed if the licence is granted.

Genocide The deliberate killing of large numbers of an ethnic, religious or national group. Genocide is defined in the Genocide Convention of 1948 as acts 'committed with intent to destroy, in whole or in part, a national, ethnical, racial or religious group'. It is this deliberate attempt to destroy a group which distinguishes it from other forms of conflict. The Genocide Convention puts an obligation on signatory states to prevent genocide and to punish its perpetrators.

Human rights A right is something which everyone is entitled to have, and a human right is something they are entitled to have simply because they are human. Human rights are set out in the Universal Declaration of Human Rights (1948), agreed by the UN General Assembly, and in subsequent treaties. States which have signed these treaties have an obligation to make these rights part of their national laws. People whose rights are being denied them can go to the courts in their country for redress. However, if the legal system in that country does not function properly, they may not be able to enforce their rights.

Internally displaced person Someone who has fled their home because of war, natural disaster or human rights abuse but has not crossed an international border.

Mediation The process of someone not involved in a dispute leading discussions between countries or different groups in order to help produce agreement.

Militia A group of people who have gathered into organised armed bands to fight for a particular cause but are not part of the regular army.

Munitions Technical term often used to describe weapons and explosives

Nation A group of people who share a common history, usually as a political entity. They are likely to have the same culture and traditions and probably the same language, although a nation's official language might be a *lingua franca* used so that none of the indigenous languages are given priority.

Nationalism The idea of the nation as a common identity for the people who belong to it. Nationalism can be a positive or neutral concept, when its advocates demand simply the right to self-determination and pride in their own language(s) or culture. In its more negative form, nationalism emphasises the superiority of one nation over another. Whatever form it takes, nationalism must answer the question of who belongs to a particular nation and what belonging to that nation means.

Negotiation Negotiation is the process by which agreements are reached in a non-violent manner. It usually involves a mediator and compromise. The countries involved in the discussion will try to reach an agreement by talking through the key points of the conflict.

Paramilitary People organised as a military force but not part of the army, often acting against government or occupiers.

Refugee In everyday speech, someone who has fled to another country. Under international law, a refugee is someone who has fled to another country and has been given refugee status by the government of the new country 'owing to a well-founded fear of being persecuted for reasons of race, religion, nationality, membership of a particular social group or political opinion'.

Small arms Small arms are designed for personal use; light weapons are designed for use by several people serving as a crew. Small arms include revolvers and self-loading pistols; rifles and carbines; sub-machine guns; assault rifles; and light machine guns.

South In this book the term 'the South' means low- and middle-income countries in Asia, Latin America and the Middle East.

State A nation or territory considered as an organised political community under one government. Most states contain two or more national or ethnic groups.

Sustainable development Meeting the needs of the present generation without harming the ability of future generations to meet their needs.

Terrorism A terrorist act is any act which is intended to cause death or serious injury to a civilian, or to any other person not taking an active part in the hostilities in a situation of armed conflict. The purpose of a terrorist act is to intimidate a population or to compel a government or international organisation to do, or abstain from doing, something.

Weapons of mass destruction Also known as WMD, these are weapons designed to kill the largest numbers of people possible and do not distinguish between civilians and military targets. The types of weapons considered to be in this class are nuclear, chemical or biological missiles and bombs.

Resources and further reading

Many of the publications in this list are available from *Oxfam's Catalogue for Schools*, a copy of which can be obtained free of charge from Oxfam (tel: 0870 333 2700; e-mail: education@ oxfam.org.uk). You can browse the catalogue online and order resources at **www.oxfam.org.uk/coolplanet/catalogue**.

Reports produced by Oxfam can either be ordered from Oxfam (telephone number as above; or online at **www.oxfam.org.uk/ publications**) at a charge of around £5 or downloaded free of charge in pdf format from **www.oxfam.org.uk** (click on 'resources' or use the search engine). Several other reports and briefing papers are available at this web address.

Background reading

The Atlas of War and Peace, Dan Smith, Earthscan, 2003

This reference book looks beyond the headlines and provides a global overview of the causes and consequences of war today and the dynamics of peacemaking. Using maps, graphics, text and up-to-date statistics, it analyses current wars and covers such key issues as: the causes of war; international terrorism; US power; the role of the UN; peace treaties; the arms trade; death tolls; refugees; landmines; child soldiers; oil, power and war; war crimes and the law; AIDS and conflict; and peace building.

A Curriculum for Global Citizenship, Oxfam, new edition 2005

What is global citizenship, and how can it be taught in UK schools? This 12-page booklet gives information about global citizenship, including the origins of the concept, its relevance to the lives of young people and a suggested framework for teaching and learning. It contains examples of good practice, and encourages practitioners to question received wisdom and to develop their own ideas on the subject.

Beyond the Headlines: An agenda for action to protect civilians in neglected conflicts, Amelia Bookstein, Oxfam, 2003

This report explains how civilians – especially those in forgotten conflicts – are suffering as a result of humanitarian aid following political priorities rather than the greatest need.

Cambodia, Ian Brown, Oxfam, 2000

This country profile explores the rich cultural heritage of Cambodia, focusing on the real lives of ordinary people and the major development issues that affect them. There are personal testimonies from six Cambodian families whose lives have been shaped by the past 30 years of conflict.

Development, Women, and War: Feminist perspectives, ed. Haleh Afshar and Deborah Eade, (Development in Practice Readers), Oxfam, 2003

The shared experiences of women, and their potential to contribute both to war and particularly to peace, are highlighted in this discussion of long-running conflicts in the Middle East, Africa, and Eastern Europe in this selection of essays.

The No-Nonsense Guide to the Arms Trade, Gideon Burrows, New Internationalist, 2002

The arms trade brings death and destruction to millions of people around the world, many of them civilians. Yet most weapons are made in countries which are members of the UN Security Council. This book exposes the characteristics of today's arms trade – cynicism, insider deals, bribery and political back-scratching – and looks at the sale of torture equipment to some of the world's worst regimes. Its chilling insights inspire and challenge.

The No-Nonsense Guide to Terrorism, Jonathan Barker, New Internationalist, 2003

Since 11 September 2001 the propaganda uses of the word 'terrorism' have multiplied, and it has never been clearer that one person's terrorist is another's freedom fighter. This book gets behind the causes and contexts of terrorism more broadly.

Shattered Lives: The case for tough international arms control, Debbie Hillier and Brian Wood, Oxfam and Amnesty International, 2003

This report gives the facts and arguments about the arms trade. It explains why there is an arms crisis and what can be done to stop it. The report shows why Oxfam, Amnesty International, and the International Action Network on Small Arms (IANSA) have together launched an international campaign calling for effective arms controls to make people genuinely safer from the threat of armed violence.

Twin Terrors – New Internationalist No. 340, November 2001

A special issue of the monthly magazine looking at issues raised by the events of 11 September 2001. There are articles, facts and figures which explore the impact of the attacks and aspects of peace and justice.

There is more information on **www.newint.org**.

Teacher's handbooks and other learning resources

Creative Force: Arts-base exercises for work with young people on issues of violence, (Save the Children UK), 2001

A look at key issues around young people and violence including: verbal violence, bullying, peer pressure, sexist and racist violence, and domestic violence. Using an arts-based approach, the resource explores questions such as: 'why do people use violence?' and 'is violence always wrong?'

Freedom! (Amnesty International UK/Hodder & Stoughton), 2001

Explores a wide range of human rights topics including the origins of human rights, women's rights, racism and identity based discrimination, genocide, censorship and pressure groups. There is also a section on the work of Amnesty International.

Get Global! A skills-based approach to active global citizenship. Key stages 3&4, ActionAid, 2003

> *Get Global!* is a guide for teachers of 11–16 year olds on how to facilitate and assess active global citizenship. It provides a structure for students to manage their own learning: from thinking about issues that are important to them, planning and participating in action, to reflecting on their performance. Innovative activities promote a skills-based (rather than content-based) approach so they can be used within different subject areas and ages.
>
> The guide is also available in pdf format, either in English or Welsh, to download from **www.oxfam.org.uk/coolplanet/teachers/ getglobal/index.htm**.

Global Lines: A citizenship teaching resource for secondary Schools, British Red Cross Society, 2004

> A citizenship teaching resource for secondary schools which aims to help young people understand the world around them, and in particular to understand conflict situations. It features case study material from Rwanda, Bosnia and Northern Ireland and includes resource material, photographs, activities to analyse media coverage and the role of humanitarian agencies in conflict situations.

How Do We Make Peace? (Discussing Global Issues), UNICEF, 2004

> This book and set of six photos contains activities to build awareness of issues of peace and conflict. Initiatives involving young people in Burundi, Cambodia, Northern Ireland and Scotland are described in the six case studies.

Human Rights (World Issues series), Penny Tripp, Chrysalis Children's Books, 2003

> Human rights are often taken for granted, but across the world people are still denied many basic rights. This book looks at fundamental issues of human rights today, such as what exactly human rights are, why it can be so difficult to put them into practice and what we can do to defend human rights worldwide.

Iraq: War and peace, Oxfam, 2003

> This resource was produced to help teachers unravel the mass of information on Iraq for their pupils, and to answer some of the many questions raised by the war. It includes a factfile on Iraq, arguments for and against the war, the history of Iraq's relationship with Britain, the poles of influence and power, the aftermath of the war and Iraq's future, with classroom activities including media analysis.
>
> It can be accessed online at **www.oxfam.org.uk/coolplanet/teachers/iraq/index.htm**

If the World Were a Village, David J. Smith, A & C Black, 2004

> Aiming to provoke thought and elicit questions, this book explains facts about the world's population in a simple way. It presents the whole world as a village of just 100 people. We find out that 22 speak a Chinese dialect and that 17 can't read or write. This book includes guidance on teaching activities for use in the classroom and notes for parents and teachers. It can provide a useful context for exploring conflict issues.

Images and Reality, International Broadcasting Trust/BFI, 2001

> Taking the floods in Mozambique as a case study, this video shows how television clips can be used in different subject areas and at different age levels. It looks at both the developing world and media approaches. The pack provides ideas for INSET sessions and activities for the classroom.

Terrorism, Understanding Global Issues series, (Publisher?), 2002

> This guide takes the events of 11 September 2001 as its starting point, putting them into a historical context and providing an overview of terrorism. It looks at both state terrorism and group terrorism, giving current examples from all over the world. Readers are guided through the relevant moral and political theories, and the battle of images and ideas that accompany them.

They Fought for Freedom: Nelson Mandela, Karin Pampallis, (Maskew Miller Longman), 2000

> This tells the life story of Nelson Mandela and his struggle for freedom in South Africa. Illustrated with photographs and maps, there is also a short activity section at the back, with questions and suggestions for discussion and debate.

Who Rules the World?, IBT, 2001

> An ideal resource for the citizenship curriculum raising issues relating to the world as a global community and giving real insight into the power structures that determine how international institutions behave. The two videos and accompanying booklets – one on the UN and one on the World Bank – take a probing look at the institutions. They encourage debate and creative thinking about whether they are needed, their weaknesses, constraints and dilemmas, and what we as individuals can do to influence them. The videos include footage from Rwanda, Angola, Bolivia and Uganda, and the issues raised are discussed in the booklets, with website links where relevant.

Websites

Finding resources on conflict, global issues and Citizenship

Many resources with a global dimension are featured on **www.globaldimension.org.uk**. For support, material and weblinks on Citizenship and the global dimension look at **www.citizenship-global.org.uk**.

Visit the Oxfam Cool Planet site for teachers and pupils for further information about topics in this book and some additional activities online. **www.oxfam.org.uk/coolplanet**

Amnesty International has plenty of resources for teachers with a large number of titles relating to human rights in the curriculum as well as the Universal Declaration of Human Rights. There is a section for students and how they can take actions on defending human rights, with publications written especially for young people that help explain and deal with issues relating to Human Rights. These publications include fiction. **www.amnesty.org.uk/education/resources/index.shtml**

New Internationalist magazine has a special page for teachers and students, 'Teaching Global Issues'. It brings together teaching resources and links to assist people who are learning about global issues.
www.newint.org

All the major UK NGOs produce educational resources, some of which are about conflict. Relevant sites include:
www.actionaid.org.uk (click on 'schools'),
www.cafod.org.uk/resources,
www.christian-aid.org.uk/learn/index.htm,
www.oxfam.org.uk/coolplanet
www.savethechildren.org.uk (click on 'Resources'),
www.unicef.org.uk/resources/index.asp.

Information about conflict issues

Alert Net gives information and pictures of emergency areas in the world including conflict areas.
www.alertnet.org

The BBC has a section on wars and conflicts including genocide.
www.bbc.co.uk/history/war

The Campaign Against Arms Trade website has information about the arms trade.
www.caat.org.uk

There is a huge range of source material and information on the issues of the arms trade and arms control on the Control Arms campaign website at **www.controlarms.org**.

The Imperial War Museum site is a good source of information and images.
www.iwm.org.uk

The International Red Cross has information about humanitarian issues related to conflict.
www.icrc.org/eng

Visit the main Oxfam site at **www.oxfam.org.uk** for a wealth of information about Oxfam's work in areas where there is conflict and the issues that are raised.

The Peace Pledge Union has a great deal of information on both peace issues and war. There is an education section.
www.ppu.org.uk

Peace Child International empowers young people to inform themselves and take action on major world issues. Young people will find a wealth of information and inspiration on this site.
www.peacechild.org

All the major UK NGOs have information and case studies relating to conflict on their websites. You can either select the relevant section or use the search engine.

www.action-aid.org.uk, **www.cafod.org.uk**, **www.christian-aid.org.uk**, **www.savethechildren.org.uk**, **www.unicef.org.uk**

Teaching about global issues and the media

Global Express is a magazine resource for teaching about world events and global issues in the news. Each issue contains photocopiable classroom activities, background information and analysis for pupils and teachers. Past editions have focused on conflict in the Middle East, Iraq, the attacks on 11

September 2001, protest and citizenship. Previous editions are downloadable at **www.dep.org.uk/globalexpress/index.htm**

Global News is a media awareness project with a teaching programme and classroom activities designed to encourage critical thinking about international news and how it is reported. The project uses a range of online English-language newspapers and news services from around the world as a resource for secondary teachers and students.
www.globalnews.org.uk.

Newsround: Lesson plans to help teachers use news in the classroom. There is an extensive range of lesson plans for secondary citizenship, PSHE and literacy-based activities on topical news stories including conflicts. The site also contains photo galleries for slideshows and guides that provide facts and explanations in a student-friendly format.
news.bbc.co.uk/cbbcnews/hi/teachers/default.stm

PBS is a private, non-profit media enterprise owned and operated by the USA's 350 public television stations. The Newshour site contains resources and lesson plans including 'World Media: Students analyse the similarities, differences and bias in world media coverage of the Iraq War' and 'The Role of the United Nations'.
www.pbs.org/newshour/extra/teachers

Teaching controversial issues in Citizenship

Citizenship Pieces, an educational site based in the London Borough of Tower Hamlets, features advice and guidance on teaching about war and terrorism, which suggests how teachers can deal with the controversies of war and the 'war against terrorism' and includes classroom strategies, the role of the teacher. whole school approaches and lesson ideas.
www.citizenship-pieces.org.uk

News media

The internet presents boundless possibilities but one of the most useful aspects is the facility to access newspapers from around the world online. Many countries produce an English language daily. Try **www.transnational.org/new/TNN.html** as a gateway to news and information media around the world. You can also try **www.onlinenewspapers.com**.

You can find articles from the press in African countries at **http://allafrica.com**.

Most of the websites of UK newspapers and news magazines have search engines which will allow users to find articles on a particular topic. Searching on 'conflict' should unearth informative and interesting material. Sites include **www.guardian.co.uk**, **www.independent.co.uk**, **www.telegraph.co.uk**, **www.timesonline.co.uk**.

The BBC News website features material from all over the world, plus features such as country profiles, specialist sections and photos.
http://news.bbc.co.uk

One World at **www.oneworld.net** has extensive news coverage of global and development issues with a large archive of articles by topic or country.